Discovering Your Dream

Contents

Preface

God has a dream for each one of us. God has planted desires in the depths of our hearts that expand our hearts and open new possibilities in our lives. God's dream for us is a passion within us that will allow for no substitute, and this dream is a restlessness that will find rest only in God. Discovering this dream will give shape and meaning to our lives and lead us to contribute to God's hopes and desires for the world, which we call the kingdom of God.

The challenge of our lives is to discover, name, and embrace that dream. Throughout our lives, God brings that dream to life and purifies it and finally confirms it. The search for that dream is a journey of hope and humility, because we know, after all, that fulfilling the dream is not our achievement but the work of God within us. No matter how halting our steps or how many detours we take or side roads we travel, we know that God walks with us and leads us to live out our dream.

The dream that God envisions for us calls us to freedom and generosity and ultimately invites us to surrender to God's love and grace. We begin our lives with adolescent dreams that often slip away as we settle for more immediate goals, but within us there is a deeper call to be a disciple and labor alongside Jesus.

This book is a simple guide to discovering the dream in each of us. This guide mines the riches of the Spiritual Exercises of St. Ignatius of Loyola. Ignatius was a dreamer, and God led him in surprising ways to a dream beyond all his hopes and expectations. Ignatius said that God taught him as a schoolmaster teaches a child. He left us a journal of his own path of discovery about God and God's dream for him, and ultimately for all of us.

This book begins with the story of Ignatius's discovery of God's dream for him, which became Ignatius's dream for his own life. Further chapters explore the basic truths that are the foundation of our dreams and our relationship with God, rooted in a call to discipleship and friendship with Jesus. The final chapters present the meaning and process of discernment, which offers us a way to hear God's voice within us and in our world and to discover our own dream, a dream planted in our hearts by God.

1

Ignatius the Dreamer

The spirituality of Ignatius is rooted in his experience of God. Ignatius didn't learn about spirituality from a book. It grew from his own experience and his reflection on his experiences, especially in what are called his pilgrim years—the time between his conversion and his founding of the Society of Jesus.

During this time, Ignatius was a layman. He wrote the Spiritual Exercises long before he ever thought of founding a religious community. The first people to make the Exercises were laypeople. Some of them decided to band together with Ignatius to form the Society of Jesus, but many did not, and they pursued many callings and ways of life. Ignatian spirituality is a spirituality for people who are trying to find God in their life experience in the world around them. It's not a spirituality for fleeing the world. It's not a spirituality unique to Jesuits. It's a spirituality for people like us today.

Ignatian spirituality is practical, not theoretical. It comes directly from Ignatius's own experiences, so let's look at his life.

A Wounded Soldier

Ignatius was born in 1491 in Spain to a noble Basque family, the youngest of thirteen children. The Loyola family prided itself on great military exploits. One of his brothers had sailed with Christopher Columbus. The family had a great sense of the dramatic, and they had a great fidelity to the king, but they remained very close to the common people. The values that were important to the family were loyalty and courage.

Don't think of Ignatius as one of those people who comes out of the womb with his hands folded in praise of God. He was a normal young Basque man at the time. His faith was pretty mediocre. As he said himself, he inherited the faith as a part of his identity. He had certain devotions he practiced, but as he admits, he had no real inner life. He also loved the good life. He loved singing and dancing and parties. At least once he and his brothers were arrested and brought to trial for causing a riot in their little town.

•

Ignatius was very tenacious and very courageous, with a desire to do great deeds and to be famous and well known. He said that his greatest temptation was to vanity. He wanted to be esteemed and admired. He wanted to become a great knight and win the hand of a lady.

At the age of fifteen Ignatius was sent to the court of King Ferdinand of Castile to train to be a diplomat, a sportsman, an officer, and a gentleman. It was a world of etiquette and courtly manners, a very superficial kind of world. He learned fencing, dancing, and singing. He read many romance novels about knights and ladies.

Ignatius lost his job at the court when his patron died, so he became a soldier in the service of a duke and a viceroy. We think of Ignatius as a military man, but he was not an astute military leader. His great challenge came during battle in the city of Pamplona, where he commanded a garrison of five hundred men under attack by an army of ten thousand French soldiers. The wise move would have been to surrender, but Ignatius tried to defend the city. He kept fighting until he was hit in the leg with a cannonball, which smashed his knee. At that, his men lost heart, and they surrendered.

The French were impressed by Ignatius's great courage, so they carried him on a stretcher back to Loyola, the castle where he had grown up. There, his sister-in-law, Magdalena, who had actually raised him since he was five years old, nursed him back to health over a period of a year.

The Dream Is Born

Ignatius's life took a new direction while he was recovering from his wounds. Ignatius was a great dreamer. He said he could go for hours imagining himself as a knight winning the hand of a lady. In fact, there was a real lady of high nobility far above his station whom he fancied. The hope of his life was to impress her by doing something dramatic. This was such a passion in his life that he was willing to suffer almost anything for it. His broken leg had been set badly; a bone stuck out, ruining his dashing appearance, so he had the doctors break the bone and reset it—without any anesthetic. He was a man who was very committed to carrying out his dream.

Ignatius spent a year recovering. He called for books, but there were only two books in the library at Loyola—a life of Christ and a collection of stories about saints. So he picked up those books and started reading.

These two books were very significant in shaping Ignatius's whole vision of the world. The first was Ludolph of Saxony's *Life of Christ*. The book took him through the events of Christ's life with pictures, and it appealed to his imagination. It also invited Ignatius to reflect and pray. Ignatian contemplation grew out of the time that Ignatius spent reading this book. Ignatius then did something else. He started daydreaming about being with Jesus and doing great things with Jesus. This fit right in with his way of approaching things. God knew how to get hold of him. This book stirred up Ignatius's desire to love and imitate Jesus. He wanted to know Jesus better, and he wanted to contemplate his own life and think about the events in his life.

Then Ignatius picked up *Lives of the Saints*. The prologue said that the saints in the book were the knights of God. *That* was something Ignatius could identify with. The knights of God did great deeds, and the lady Mary was in the picture, too, which excited Ignatius. He read about St. Dominic and said, "I could do better than that!" He read about St. Francis of Assisi: "I can do better than that!" Ignatius dreamed of becoming the greatest saint of all.

Becoming a saint caught his imagination, it caught his energy, and it caught his passion. He began to notice that when he would spend all day dreaming about being a knight and winning the hand of a lady, he later grew sad, empty, and frustrated. When he contemplated the life of Christ and thought about being a great saint, he was filled with peace, a sense of wholeness, and a sense of harmony and joy. He said,

"What does this mean? What's going on with these different feelings?"

A new dream was born. To Ignatius, the peace he felt after dreaming of following Christ meant that this was the direction God wanted him to go. The great knight who wanted to win the hand of a lady was to become a great saint, a knight of God, and to do great things for God. He had a new dream.

The Dream Is Purified

But Ignatius's dream needed refinement and purification. He didn't know very much about how to pray or how to find the path he should take. Ignatius tells a story about himself that shows just how much refinement he needed.

Right after his conversion he set out on his donkey for the Benedictine abbey of Montserrat. A man rode with him for a while. The man was a Moor, a Muslim, and they talked about Mary, the mother of God. In the Moor's tradition Mary was a virgin when she gave birth to Jesus, but she didn't stay a virgin. Ignatius became very upset, because he felt that the man was insulting his new lady, Mary. The Moor got tired of Ignatius and rode off. Ignatius sat on his donkey and wondered, "What am I supposed to do? As a loyal knight I should go kill that man because he insulted my lady. But now I'm a Christian, and Christians probably don't do things like that."

So Ignatius decided to leave the decision up to the donkey. The road split into two. One route would take him into the city, where he would follow the Moor and kill him. The other route led down the highway. Ignatius let go of the reins, and the donkey took him away from the Moor.

Ignatius told that story to show how immature he was at that stage of his life. Although he was committed to follow the Lord and to be part of God's great plan, he didn't know how to do it. Ignatius needed the gift of discernment. Discernment is the ability to discover God's will in the movements that happen within our own hearts and the events of our lives. It helps us answer important questions. What is God calling me to? Where is God leading me? And where is God not leading me?

Ignatius's journey of purification continued. He went to the Benedictine monastery of Montserrat to begin his pilgrimage to Jerusalem. At the altar of Our Lady, he laid his sword down and said, "I will now become your knight." As he was leaving the monastery, he exchanged clothes with a beggar so he could live a poor life.

Ignatius decided to stop for a few days in a little town called Manresa so he could jot down some notes about what he had experienced. As it turns out, instead of a few days, he spent almost a year in Manresa. And this is where his dream of following God was purified. At Manresa, Ignatius said, "God dealt with me the way a schoolmaster deals with a child." He didn't know anything about the spiritual life, so God taught him. It was that experience that shaped his life, and it was out of that experience that the book *Spiritual Exercises* was born.

At first, Ignatius was filled with enthusiasm. He prayed seven hours a day and loved every minute of it. He would go around town and grab people and sit with them in the square and tell them about God. He helped out in the hospital. He was experiencing God in profound ways. He also did great penances, too many penances. He harmed his health and later realized these strenuous penances were imprudent for him.

But then after about three months, the bottom fell out. Ignatius was filled with darkness and desolation. He said he didn't want to pray anymore. He went to the Eucharist, and he said it meant nothing. Suddenly, God seemed very distant, and Ignatius grew discouraged. A voice in his head said, "Who do you think you are? Look at the first thirty years of your life. You're not going to be a great saint. You can't keep this up. Sure you can keep this up for a few weeks or a few months, but you know, you've got another thirty or forty years to go. You are not going to be able to keep doing this." Ignatius became so depressed that he entertained suicidal thoughts.

Gradually, Ignatius emerged from his depression. He went through a time of purification like many of the great saints did. He had mystical experiences. He had visions of creation, of the Trinity, and of the presence of Christ in the Eucharist.

One vision is particularly important to the purification of his dream, and this vision is key to understanding the whole Ignatian perspective. The vision took place in the town of Manresa, on the banks of the river Cardoner. While sitting by the river one day, Ignatius had an experience of God. He said it was more of an intellectual understanding than something you could see. He said it gave him a profound clarity about God as one and as three, the Trinity of God. It was an experience of the world as a gift from God, coming down from above, and of all things going back to God. That is the sweep of human history: God coming down, and everything returning to God. The two great moments in history were creation, when God created the world, and the Incarnation, when God took on human flesh. After this vision, Ignatius always looked at life and the world around him as a gift coming from a loving God that is on its way back to God.

Seeing in a New Way

The vision at the river Cardoner had three important consequences for Ignatius. First, he surrendered to God's grace. He realized that he wasn't going to be a great saint on his own. Becoming a saint would have to be a work of God—of God leading him, guiding him, sustaining him, strengthening him. Interestingly, after this experience at the river he didn't ever talk again about being a great saint. He had to let God do within him what God wanted to do within him.

The second consequence was that Ignatius began to think of himself as something other than a solitary pilgrim. At the river he realized that God was calling him to be a person of the church, of the whole Christian community. And God was calling him "to help souls"—to help people, to share the vision with them, to be of service to other people.

Finally, Ignatius began to think of Christ in a new way. He saw Christ as a leader of the process of bringing the world back to God. Christ was laboring in the world to make that happen. The risen Christ in our midst is struggling to bring the world back to God. Ignatius's call was to labor alongside Christ to bring the world back to God. He was to be part of this great plan, the work of salvation.

But the purification wasn't finished. There was much more to come.

2

The Dream Is Realized

After his time in Manresa, Ignatius went to Jerusalem, thinking that this is what God wanted him to do. He thought that it was God's will for him to spend his life there. When he arrived, the Franciscans in charge of the holy places were alarmed. Many European pilgrims were being kidnapped by bandits and held for ransom. The Franciscans ordered Ignatius to leave the city. Ignatius objected; he said that God had wanted him to go to Jerusalem. But the Franciscan superior told him, "If you don't leave, I'm going to excommunicate you from the church." So Ignatius left. Clearly, God had something else for him to do.

So Ignatius moved to plan B. He spent most of his life on plan Bs. His plan As seldom worked out.

Ignatius thought he should preach and teach in Europe, but to do that he needed an education. So he had to go back to school and start at the beginning. He went to school with young boys to learn Latin, because to get into the university, people had to learn Latin. After that, he went to two Spanish universities before finally arriving at the University of Paris. He eventually graduated with a master's degree.

Companions for the Journey

In Paris, something very significant happened. Ignatius met some other students who were much younger than he was. This group of students included Francis Xavier, who would later become St. Francis Xavier, and Peter Faber, who would later become Blessed Peter Faber. Ignatius began to tell his new friends about his experience of God, and he guided them through his Spiritual Exercises. Eventually, Ignatius and six other men decided that they wanted to serve God together. They had a common vision; they shared Ignatius's vision, his experience. They took vows of poverty and chastity, but they still didn't think of themselves as a religious order or a religious community. They decided to go as a group to Jerusalem.

They never got to Jerusalem; the boats couldn't sail because of the ongoing wars. They had a plan B: if they couldn't go to the Holy Land, they would present themselves to the pope and let him use them as he wished. They told the pope they would go anywhere. When the pope agreed, the seven companions decided that they needed to make a more definite commitment to one another. They began a process of discernment that ended with a decision to become a religious order.

The Dream Confirmed

On a journey to Rome, Ignatius and two of his companions stopped at a little chapel called La Storta, a wayside chapel popular with pilgrims. It was just a small place to stop and pray. Ignatius prayed for a while and had another extraordinary experience of God.

He sensed God saying that he was going to be good to Ignatius in Rome. He had a vision of the Father and Jesus, and Jesus was carrying his cross. The Father said to Jesus, "Son, I want you to take this man, Ignatius, to work with you." Jesus turned to Ignatius and said, "I want you to come and labor alongside me." That was the call Ignatius had wanted all his life. This was the confirmation that he was on the right path, that he was following what God wanted him to do.

Confirmation is the final essential step in a process of discernment. You make a decision, then you bring it to God and live with that decision for a while. If it's the right decision, your heart finally says, "Yes, this is right." This is what

Ignatius felt at La Storta: God saying, "Yes, this is right." What he heard from Jesus was, "I want you to serve us," meaning Father, Son, and Holy Spirit. "I want you to help people. I want you to labor alongside me." This was the grace Ignatius had been seeking for fifteen years. "Am I on the right path? Is this what God wants me to do?" And God said, "Yes, go to Rome. That is the right path."

Acceptance and Community

Some very important things came out of the vision at La Storta. The first was a profound sense of the Father placing Ignatius at the side of the Son. Ignatius and his companions would labor with Jesus to bring the world back to the Father. That was the whole vision of his life, the value of his life, the driving force in his life—to bring the world back to God.

This vision at La Storta brought Ignatius a sense of the Trinity having accepted him, saying, "Yes, we want you to work with us." It was very significant to Ignatius that, in his vision, Christ was carrying his cross; he realized that laboring alongside Jesus was not going to be easy. He would serve, but it would be in poverty, in humility, and facing a lot of opposition. There would be a lot of suffering along the way.

Ignatius said that the La Storta vision was an experience of community. What he had discovered at the river Cardoner was confirmed at the chapel. He was to serve with others, not alone. The community around Ignatius became the Society of Jesus.

Ignatius also said that the name of Jesus became very important to him at La Storta. When it came time to name the religious order he founded, Ignatius chose the Society of Jesus. It wouldn't be named after him, as the Dominicans were named after St. Dominic and the Franciscans after St. Francis. People objected. They said his order couldn't be the Society of Jesus because everybody is a follower of Jesus. But Ignatius said, "God told me at La Storta that we are the Society of Jesus." Now Ignatius was a Basque, with a reputation of being a stubborn person. Whenever others would question an idea of his, he would say after a while that he saw it at the river Cardoner or at La Storta. And that would end the debate.

Finally at La Storta, Ignatius received a deep sense of connection to Rome. His order would be connected to the church and in service to the church. This became very important to him and to the Society of Jesus.

Coming Out God's Door

I've described three moments in Ignatius's life in which he experienced God in very different ways. The first, at Loyola, came through the reading of books. God gradually led

Ignatius to let go of his dream of being a great knight and to embrace what he was able to embrace at that moment—a dream of following God and doing great things. But that dream had to be purified. Ignatius had to let go of the adolescent part, the immature part, the sense of "I can do it all on my own." He had to understand that the dream was for others. It was a vision he had to share. He had to help souls. He had to bring other people to the same vision of God. Finally there was that moment when God confirmed the decision and told Ignatius, "This is what I want you to do; this is who you are."

Ignatius later would use the phrase "always go in their door and come out your own." God went in Ignatius's door and led him out another. God went in the door of Ignatius's dream of becoming a great knight and led Ignatius to a whole new dream, a whole new vision.

For Ignatius, his vision meant being able to adapt to circumstances. He wanted to go to Jerusalem. He got sent back. He wanted to go to Jerusalem the second time. That didn't work. Then he wanted to be sent to other continents to do great missionary work. Instead, his brothers made him the superior general of the Society of Jesus, and he spent the last fifteen years of his life sitting at a desk writing letters and writing the constitutions of the Society of Jesus. That was not

Ignatius's plan. It was God's plan. The grace was that he was open to God's plan and found God in it.

The main catalyst of change in Ignatius's life was experience, not what people told him or what he read. Experience is what brought about change in his life. God dealt with Ignatius in a very direct, personal way. He experienced God at work in his life and in all the events of his life. His wisdom came not from textbooks but from his reflection on his experiences. He noticed how God was working in his heart. That's the gift Ignatius teaches to us in the Spiritual Exercises.

What Ignatius's Dream Has to Do with You

Ignatian spirituality leads us to notice and to reflect on our personal experience. God touches each one of us. At the heart of Ignatian spirituality is Ignatius's belief that God touches each individual's soul. We need only to notice it, to listen for it, and to follow it. That was Ignatius's own experience of God and his experience of guiding others through the Spiritual Exercises.

Ignatius was a man with a dream. That dream was born at Loyola, purified at the river Cardoner, and confirmed at the chapel at La Storta. Ignatius also believed that God has a dream for each one of us and that God plants that dream in the depths of our hearts. Our dream is a passion within us that will allow no substitute. It's a restlessness that will find rest only in God. It is the deepest desires of our heart, the desires that will give shape and meaning to our lives. That's what Ignatius learned from his own experience.

Ignatius's own experience was the basis for the Spiritual Exercises. In them, Ignatius shows us a way to discover God's dream for us inside our own hearts, to discover our own deepest desires, and to live them out with integrity. The Spiritual Exercises are a way to come to freedom, to hear God's call as Ignatius did, and to respond in generosity and love. We'll look at the Exercises next.

3

The Spiritual Exercises

What are the Spiritual Exercises? First of all, they are an experience. They are rooted in Ignatius's life experience and in his experience of God. They are an experience for those who "make" them. In their full form, the Spiritual Exercises are an experience of thirty days of solitude, with four or five hours of prayer each day.

The Exercises are a way to encounter God. They are a process that is intended to lead us to the freedom that allows us to hear God's call and to follow that call in faith. It is the freedom to follow Jesus and to share the work of redemption.

The Spiritual Exercises are also a journey—a journey of transformation and a journey of conversion. They help us get in touch with the desires of our heart, which really are God's desires within us. It is always important to remember that when we mention the Spiritual Exercises, the first thing we are talking about is an experience that people go through.

But the *Spiritual Exercises* is also a book, a very brief book that can be read very quickly. It outlines a series of exercises; you might call them a kind of spiritual aerobic workout. They are exercises that you *do*—prayers, meditations, contemplations, methods of self-examination, guidelines for discerning God's movements in our hearts. They are exercises for discovering God's will in our lives and for making decisions. We *do* these exercises, but the content of the Spiritual Exercises is really something that God does within each individual person. The Exercises help you get in touch with what God is doing in your life. They help you experience God and see how God is working within you. Most people make the Exercises with the help of a spiritual director. The director is primarily interested in what God is doing in your heart, because that's the content of the Spiritual Exercises. You can't find that in the book. You find it in prayer and reflection on your own life.

The book *Spiritual Exercises* is written for the spiritual director who guides people through the Exercises. The book was first printed in 1548. Ignatius printed five hundred copies, and he controlled all of them. He gave copies only to people who had already made the Exercises. He allowed only people who had made the Exercises to direct someone else in them. The Exercises are an art form, not a science. They need to be adapted to each individual person according to how God is working in the heart of that person.

Ignatius's Experience of God

The *Spiritual Exercises* is a journal of Ignatius's own experience of God, starting with the year he spent at Manresa. The book shows how God purified Ignatius's dream and made clear that his call was to help souls, to be an apostolic person, to be a person of the church, and to carry on the work of Jesus. During that year Ignatius kept notes, and then he worked on the Exercises for twenty-five years. By directing other people through the Exercises, he learned what he should put in the book to help the spiritual director. But basically the *Spiritual Exercises* is a journal of his own conversion experience. It's a journal about God moving in Ignatius's heart. As he led other people through the Exercises, Ignatius discovered that his journey was really a model for everyone's journey. There are certain common patterns in the way God works with us and the way we respond to God. At the same time, each person experiences God in a unique way. That's why the Exercises had to be adapted for each individual person. They are a paradigm, a model, a pattern for God's dealing with people.

To make the Exercises, you have to experience them. You can't just read or study the book; it's a book to be prayed. You might read the whole book, but you still can't say then that you have made the Spiritual Exercises. To make the Spiritual Exercises, you need to go apart and spend some time in prayer and reflection under the guidance of a spiritual director.

The *Spiritual Exercises* is a book written by a layperson for laypeople. The experience that it records took place long before Ignatius had any idea of founding a religious community. He was a layperson trying to figure out a way to follow God. The people he first directed through the Spiritual Exercises, most of them faculty and students at the University of Paris, were laypeople. Some decided to enter religious life or go into priesthood, but many didn't. So it is important to realize that the Spiritual Exercises are not just for Jesuits, or monks, or priests, or religious. The Spiritual Exercises lay out the pattern of life for every Christian.

What to Expect

Before presenting the Exercises proper, Ignatius sets forth some guidelines that are important for understanding the Spiritual Exercises. First is a description of a "spiritual exercise." He says that a spiritual exercise is any means that helps us come into contact with God, anything—a prayer, a meditation, a reflection—that will dispose our hearts and set us free so we can find God's will in our life. He compares spiritual exercises to physical exercises: just as there are exercises that you do for your physical health, there are exercises you do for your spiritual health.

Ignatius then talks about what he hopes people will get from the Spiritual Exercises. He hopes that people will receive spiritual knowledge, not just intellectual knowledge. He is interested in felt knowledge or interior knowledge—the intimate understanding of a truth. This kind of knowledge is the difference between knowing about Jesus and knowing Jesus. It's the difference between knowing in your head that God loves you and experiencing that love in your heart. Sometimes the longest journey of life is from our head to our heart. We can say, "Yes, I know that. I know God loves me." But do we really *know* it? Do we really experience it in our hearts? The kind of knowledge Ignatius wants is the knowledge that touches the heart and transforms us, knowledge that motivates us to act in a whole new way. He is looking for an intimate, interior, felt knowledge.

Ignatius also says in these opening directives that to make the Exercises you need magnanimity. You need a "big soul." You need openness. You need generosity. You need great desires. That's what he looked for in people who were going to make the Exercises. He looked for people with big desires who wanted to do great things, people who wanted to do more. He wanted people who were not content with where they were, who were restless, and who were looking to give something more. If you're content where you are and you want to stay there and don't want to be bothered, then don't make the Spiritual Exercises. You should make them if you want a challenge to do more, to open your heart more fully to God.

There's one more important point at the beginning of the Spiritual Exercises: Ignatius says that God is the real director of the Exercises, and that he believes that the Creator and Lord communicate directly with the soul. That idea is the heart of the Exercises and the heart of Ignatius's spirituality. God touches each of our souls through our thoughts, our desires, our imaginings, and our feelings.

Before I directed a retreat myself for the first time, a very wise spiritual director walked by and said, "You look nervous." And I responded, "I *am* nervous. I've made the Exercises twice, I've done them, but now I'm going to direct them." And he told me, "It's really pretty simple. You pray for two things. Pray for the person you're directing, and then pray to stay out of the way. It's God's work; it's not yours. Stay out of the way. God will do great things."

In the Exercises the director is there only to facilitate a conversation between God and the person making the Exercises, not to tell the person something, not to teach him or her, but only to guide the person and facilitate that person's encounter with God. The Spiritual Exercises are about a personal encounter with God.

Making the Exercises

Ignatius thought that the full Exercises would take thirty days of one-on-one work with an experienced spiritual director. He also thought that a person should make the Exercises only once in his or her lifetime. Jesuit religious make them twice: when we enter the Jesuits in the novitiate and again after all our studies are over and we have been in ministry for a while, maybe fifteen or twenty years later. I first made the Spiritual Exercises when I was eighteen years old. There's nothing wrong with being eighteen, but I wasn't quite ready for the Exercises. It was a very different experience when I made them again at the age of thirty-eight.

People started adapting the Exercises even during Ignatius's lifetime. First of all, some people made them more than once. Then they made them for shorter periods of time. Eight days became the standard shortened version of the Exercises. You can't really make the full Exercises in eight days, but you can do some of the exercises and experience some of the graces. Every Jesuit makes an eight-day retreat every year as part of his own spiritual practice. Many other people now also make eight-day retreats.

Another adaptation is making the Spiritual Exercises in a group. In this way, you go to a Jesuit retreat house for a series of talks about the themes of the Exercises with a group of people. Then there's quiet time to pray and time to meet with someone who will guide you and direct you.

Another adaptation is something Ignatius envisioned himself—the Exercises in the midst of everyday life. In this context you pray for an hour every morning and meet with a spiritual director once a week for six to nine months. This is a very rich experience that allows you to integrate your prayer with your everyday life.

The Purpose of the Spiritual Exercises

There are two schools of thought regarding the purpose of the Spiritual Exercises. One is that the purpose of the Exercises is to make a life decision; the other is that the purpose is to draw close to God. Both are true. Ignatius envisioned them originally as exercises to order one's life so that one could reach an ordered decision. He saw it as a process of coming to a major life decision. But obviously, many people make the Exercises to enrich their relationship with God. They've already made a life commitment to priesthood or marriage or religious life or single life. They're trying to discover how to live out the gospel more faithfully in those circumstances.

This is how I would summarize the purposes of the Spiritual Exercises. The first is to come to freedom in order to make a decision. The Spiritual Exercises help you order your life, clarify your goals, and decide how you achieve them.

Second, they help us discover our role in the plan of salvation. What is God calling you to do in your life, and how do you fit into God's plan of salvation of the world? The Exercises help you discover where God is asking you to go.

Finally, the Exercises develop and deepen our relationship with God. They bring us closer to God, help us become more intimate with God, and let God work more deeply within our hearts so that we can draw closer to God.

The Exercises are about making decisions, but they are about making decisions out of freedom, not out of pleasure, power, or prestige. We'll see where that freedom comes from when we look at the First Principle and Foundation.

4

The First Principle and Foundation

In order to make a free decision, Ignatius says, you first have to get some basic things straight: Who is God? Who are you? How do you relate to God? What's the meaning and value of the world in which we live? To get at these questions, Ignatius offers a consideration at the beginning of the *Spiritual Exercises*, which he calls the First Principle and Foundation. It addresses the basic question of the purpose of our life and why we are here. I want to offer two versions of this. The first is the more literal translation:

> Human beings are created to praise, reverence, and serve God, our Lord, and by means of doing this to save their souls.

The other things on the face of the earth are created for human beings, to help them in the pursuit of the end for which they are created. From this it follows we ought to use these things to the extent that they help us toward our end and free ourselves from them to the extent that they hinder us from the end.

To attain this, it is necessary to make ourselves indifferent to all created things, in regard to everything which is left to our free will and is not forbidden.

Consequently, on our own part, we ought not to seek health rather than sickness, wealth rather than poverty, honor rather than dishonor, a long life rather than a short one, and so in all other matters.

Rather we ought to desire and choose only that which is more conducive to the end for which we were created.

As you can see, Ignatius makes a distinction between means and ends. The purpose and goal of life is to praise, reverence, and serve God. Everything else helps us achieve that purpose. What most of us do, however, is pick out our favorite means and make them an end. The end—loving and serving God—becomes the means. But Ignatius says that the first step is to be clear about the end; then you choose the means that is most conducive to reach the end. Your goal is to praise, reverence, and serve God, and to come to eternal life. Marriage, religious life, priesthood, single life—these are all means to get there. You don't choose one of these means and then try to work the goal around it.

Here is another version of the First Principle and Foundation, a contemporary paraphrase by David Fleming, SJ. It's a little bit easier for us to read today:

> God freely created us so that we might know, love, and serve him in this life and be happy with Him forever. God's purpose in creating us is to draw forth from us a response of love and service here on earth, so that we may obtain our goal of everlasting happiness with Him in heaven.
>
> All the things of this world are gifts from God, created for us to be the means by which we can get to know Him better, love Him more surely, and serve Him more faithfully.
>
> As a result, we ought to use and appreciate these gifts from God insofar as they help us toward our goal of loving service and union with God. But insofar as any created things hinder our progress towards our goal, we ought to let them go.
>
> In everyday life, we should keep ourselves indifferent or undecided in the face of all created gifts when we have an option and we do not have the clarity of what would be the better choice. We ought not to be led on by our natural likes and dislikes even in matters such as health or sickness, wealth or poverty, between living in the east or the west, becoming an accountant or a lawyer.

Rather, our only desire and our one choice should be that option which better leads us to the goal for which God created us.

For Ignatius, this is the starting point of the Spiritual Exercises. You have to get straight what God's plan is and who you are before God. What is the plan that God is creating within us? Ignatius offered the First Principle and Foundation as a consideration. It's not even clear how he used it. Some people think that Ignatius would get into a relationship with someone, and then spend days, weeks, even months talking about the purpose of life. When Ignatius found that the person achieved some clarity, then he would take them into the Exercises. But the First Principle and Foundation exists as an independent consideration for us to think about at the beginning of the Exercises. Let's look at the basic truths and the basic attitudes of heart that the First Principle and Foundation calls us to.

We Are Loved

The first premise is that we are created by God. We are creatures. We tend to forget that sometimes. Ignatius wants to remind us that whatever we do in the rest of the Exercises, we do it as people created by God. We're created to praise, reverence, and serve God. Therefore, we're dependent on God, not just for our original creation but also for every moment of our existence. We are continually being created by God. We are pure gift. And Ignatius says that we have to hold to that truth very firmly as we begin.

We are created out of love. We are loved by God. This is clearer in the contemporary paraphrase of the First Principle and Foundation. The experience of being loved by God is the fundamental Christian grace. Without that experience, without some belief in it, our Christian life will go astray. Our life will become a frantic attempt to win God's love. We don't have to win God's love. We are loved by God, unconditionally, from the moment of our conception.

The First Principle and Foundation invites us to see the world as a product of love. We have to affirm the goodness of the world. The first grace is to know that each one of us is a product of God's love. So we read Isaiah 43, which says, "God loves us from our mother's womb." We read Isaiah 49 that says, "We are written on the palm of his hand. Even if a mother forgets her child, God will never forget us." It is that experience of God's fidelity, God's love, and God's care for us that assures us that we are loved by God and that the world is a product of love. The world is a gift from the hands of a loving God.

We can say that in our heads, but do we believe it in our hearts? My experience in giving the Exercises and in giving people spiritual direction is that it is very difficult for some people to really believe that they are deeply, intimately, even passionately, loved by God. But that is the foundational grace out of which the rest of the Exercises flow. Without it, it's hard to continue, especially into the First Week of the Exercises, when we deal with our sin.

Blessed Peter Faber, one of the students with Ignatius at the University of Paris, wanted to make the Exercises, but Ignatius said no because he thought he wasn't ready. Peter Faber had a terrible image of God. He was terrified of God; he thought that God was a harsh judge. Ignatius made him wait for four years until he had a really profound sense that he was loved by God. Ignatius thought that this attitude of heart was the foundational grace for making the Spiritual Exercises.

In a sense, the Exercises are simply a series of ways of experiencing God's love. We experience God's love in creation, in forgiveness, in God's calling us, in God's inviting us into the paschal mystery, in God's call to eternal life. It's one long love story. That's why this foundational grace is very important.

Getting Free

The second grace of the First Principle and Foundation is to see everything we experience as a gift from God. Everything is a gift to be used to praise God, to reverence God, to serve God, to serve one another, to love other people. Ignatius says, "To attain this, it is necessary to make ourselves indifferent to all created things." *Indifferent* is not the best of words for us, because *indifferent* means not caring, as in "You pick the restaurant tonight, Chinese or Italian—I'm indifferent." That's not what Ignatius means by *indifferent*. He means that we are so passionately committed to God and to following God and God's plan that everything else is secondary to that one goal and that one purpose. We say, "I will put anything else aside. I'm indifferent. I'm at balance and equilibrium." The only question for us to ask is whether something will bring us closer to God or not. Ignatius talks about the spiritual director and the one making the Exercises being at equilibrium so that they can choose what is more conducive to God's will. Indifference is a preference for God and God's plan that embraces everything we do.

A better word than *indifferent* is *freedom*. We need to be free to choose what gives greater glory to God. Many things capture our hearts; many things can keep us from being free enough to hear God's call in our life. We hold back. We say to God, "I will do anything as long as I don't have to let go of *this* particular thing." That's what Ignatius would call a disordered attachment, something your heart is wrapped around and something that is wrapped around your heart. You're not free to hear the call to something new or something different in your life.

The Spiritual Exercises are all about achieving freedom. Ignatius believed that once you are truly free, the rest is simple. The decisions become clear. You know what to do. The challenge is to get free, to get to that place of balance where you say, "Wherever you call me, God, I will go." Teilhard de Chardin called this passionate indifference. We all need to have passionate indifference, to be so committed to God and God's project. Everything else we can take or leave, depending on whether it brings us to that goal. This freedom is the freedom to make a commitment.

All Is Gift

There is always a temptation to take things for granted, to lose the sense that everything we have is a gift from God. We can keep a sense of giftedness by staying in touch with the Giver. Something ceases to be a gift when we make it our own, when we claim it, wrap our hands around it, and say, "This is mine."

I'll give you a humbling example from my own life. About fifteen years ago, I had to move. I had been in the place a long time, and so I had a lot of stuff to pack. I wanted to throw some things away. I was ordained in 1969, and in the 1970s, whenever you gave a retreat or a talk, somebody would always give you a candle, or a stole, or a statue. These things were all very meaningful at the time. When I came to move, I had all these things that tied me to wonderful experiences over the years. But then, looking at them as I packed, I realized I didn't know where a particular candle came from. I'm sure it signified a very significant and touching moment in which God was present, but now I didn't remember the moment. Then I went to the next candle. This time I remembered where that candle came from. I remembered that retreat, and the person who gave it to me.

I started making two piles: one for stoles and candles and things that I couldn't remember, and another pile for those for which I remembered the occasion and the person. I sat down and looked at them and said, "The things in the first pile are possessions, and the things in the second pile are gifts." The gifts were connected to a giver. I knew who gave them to me. I still experience them as a gift. The things in the other pile are now just possessions. So I got rid of the possessions and kept the gifts.

The First Principle and Foundation is trying to remind us that everything in our life is a gift from the hands of a loving God. Everything is given to us. When we start taking something for granted, when we start making it a possession, we lose touch with the Giver.

Gratitude and Trust

The First Principle and Foundation calls us to gratitude. Ignatius told a friend that ingratitude was the greatest sin. As a matter of fact, ingratitude is the source of all sin, because when we take something and misuse it, when we take something and claim it as our own, we destroy it as a gift. We fail to recognize the Giver.

The second call of the First Principle and Foundation is to trust. If you believe that there's a giver who will always keep giving, then you don't have to cling to things, because you are going to get more gifts. We are called to open our hands and trust the Giver, because the Giver is faithful. Share the gift because the Giver will give you more. That sense of trust, that sense that God cares for us, leads to freedom.

Finally, the First Principle and Foundation is a call to stewardship. If all we have are gifts, then we're to nourish, cherish, and share them. That's why God gives us our gifts. The moment we start hoarding our gifts, and not sharing them, the moment we neglect them, we no longer see them as gifts from the hands of a giver.

The First Principle and Foundation tells us of the wonders of creation and the giftedness of life. It calls us to gratitude, to freedom, so that we can make love- and life-filled decisions. The freedom comes from knowing that you're loved and gifted. That's what sets our heart free. It is the freedom to find God in our experience and in the world around us. It is the freedom that comes from experiencing at a very deep, personal level that we are loved by God.

This is what Ignatius saw in his vision at the river Cardoner. There he saw the whole world as a gift from God and on its way back to God. Ignatius's vision—an image of the giftedness of the world and the giftedness of our lives, a vision that invites us to respond freely in love—stayed with Ignatius all his life.

5

The Dynamics of the Exercises

The First Principle and Foundation provides the essential grounding for the Spiritual Exercises. We are created, we are dependent, and we are loved by God. It affirms that we are created by God out of love. We desire to make decisions that draw us closer to God. With that, the Spiritual Exercises proper begin.

The Exercises are divided into four "weeks." These are not seven-day weeks; rather, they are stages of growth in our relationship with God. The stages are (1) an experience of being loved by God unconditionally, (2) an experience of being forgiven, (3) an experience of being called to be a disciple of Jesus, and (4) an experience of entering into the Christian mystery of the dying and rising of Jesus. The four weeks take us through this process. They invite us to conversion, to a sense of vocation, and to purification and deeper union with God. This is the history of personal salvation that God desires for each of us. It is Christian life. It is Christian salvation.

Ignatius gives us a series of "exercises"—meditations, considerations, and contemplations. Some of these engage the intellect. Some are more affective. Some are very imaginative because Ignatius wants to elicit very deep feelings about who we are and who God is. He wants us to have a felt knowledge of God and of our own great and generous desires. He does not want to impose anything on us. He believes that our desires for God, for forgiveness, and to follow Jesus are already within us. Through the Spiritual Exercises he wants to help us get in touch with those desires. He wants to cut through all our superficial desires to get to the deeper desire in our hearts that God planted there.

At the beginning of each exercise, Ignatius names a grace for you to pray for. At the end of every exercise, he invites you to a "colloquy," a conversation with God. The grace and this conversation are the heart of the Exercises. These will be the focus as we discuss the dynamics of the Exercises. When looking at the Spiritual Exercises, we see the process and the dynamic: the grace you pray for and the kind of conversation that you are invited to. We'll see that as we go through the Exercises.

The First Week: Being Forgiven

The First Week flows out of the sense of being loved that we experience in the First Principle and Foundation. The Foundation puts us in touch with God's love and the giftedness of our lives. We become aware of the great debt that we owe to God for our very existence and for the invitation to eternal life and salvation. We know that our response to that should be praise, reverence, thanksgiving, and great trust in God.

At some point, after reflecting on the Foundation for a while, most people realize that they haven't responded very well to God's love. We get in touch with the inadequacies of our responses, our lack of gratitude, our rejection of God's love, our sinfulness, our brokenness, and the way we have taken God's gifts and made them possessions.

We then begin to confront sin. For Ignatius, sin is disorder in our relationship with God and with one another. It is not following the plan. It is getting things out of sync and out of place. Sin for Ignatius is ingratitude. Every sin derives from taking the gift for granted and misusing it, from throwing the gift away, from taking the gift and not sharing it.

Ignatius is not that concerned with all the particulars of sin; for him, sin is not just an action that we do. Sin is ingratitude. Sin for him is unfreedom. It is the disordered attachments that we hang on to, the things that enslave us, and the things that get in the way of our service to God and our love of God and one another.

In the First Week, Ignatius invites us first of all to reflect on the history of sin. He has us look at the fall of the angels, at the Adam and Eve story, and at our own story. He wants us to get a sense that we are not alone. We think, "I'm not the first one to sin. I didn't make up sin. I was born into a history of sin." There is a salvation history, but there is also a history of sinfulness that we are born into. Ignatius wants us to reflect on that and then to realize that we are a part of that history.

Ignatius has a second theme. He doesn't want us to focus only on sin. He wants us to focus on the mercy of God, on God's forgiving love in Jesus. So the grace that we pray for in this first stage of the Exercises is the grace to experience ourselves as loved sinners. We are sinners. We are broken. We are at times ungrateful. We are at times selfish. But we are loved. As Paul says in the letter to the Romans, "He loved us even when we were sinners."

The experience of the First Week is that of being loved as a sinner. We become aware that we need a savior and that we have a savior in Jesus. We have the grace to see ourselves as God sees us. This is hard to do. Often we are very hard on ourselves. Ignatius wants us to see the mercy and love of God. So we pray for sorrow. We pray for a profound gratitude for God's mercy and God's forgiveness. We are confronted with our sinfulness, our helplessness, our need for God, and our need for salvation. But even more, we are confronted with the overwhelming goodness and mercy of God.

Ignatius then invites us to have a conversation with Jesus at the foot of the cross. He asks us to imagine Christ our Lord suspended on the cross before us and to converse with him in a very open, intimate way. We ask him how, even though he is the Creator, he has become a human being. How did that happen? Why did he do that? How is it that he passed from eternal life to death here in time, and how did he come to die in this way for my sins? It's very personal. Jesus didn't die for sins in general; he died for the sins of each one of us. We are astonished and filled with wonder at the realization that he died for our individual sins.

In a similar way, Ignatius wants us to reflect on ourselves and ask three questions: In light of this love that created me, that forgives me, that calls me to life, what have I done for Christ? What am I doing for Christ? What ought I do for Christ? Ignatius always asked the question, what do I *do*? It is not enough to have a wonderful experience. The question is, what am I called to *do*? This spirituality is of action, of going forth to do something. That question will stay with each one of us throughout the Exercises: "What ought I to do? What is my call? What is my vocation? What is God asking me to do?"

Ignatius then invites us to gaze on Jesus hanging on the cross and to speak whatever comes to our minds. He doesn't tell us what to say. He says, "It's you and the Lord. Speak whatever comes to your mind. Say whatever you want to say, and then listen to what the Lord wants to say to you."

The grace of the First Week is becoming filled with gratitude because of God's faithful love even in the face of our infidelity. That's the First Week. It's not an easy week. It is challenging but ultimately very consoling.

The Second Week: Being Called

The sense of being loved and forgiven opens our hearts and sets us free to hear God's call. There's a connection. Gratitude expands our hearts. Gratitude fills us with a desire to share this good news. We want to tell other people that God loves us and that God forgives us. Gratitude is contagious. It opens us to service.

There are two wonderful stories in the New Testament showing this connection between forgiveness and service.

They both involve St. Peter. The first story is about Peter and Jesus and the other disciples fishing. As usual, Peter catches nothing. (Someone once commented that in Scripture Peter never catches a fish without it being a miracle.) Jesus tells Peter to cast the net on the other side, and suddenly the boat is filled with fish.

How does Peter respond? He realizes that there's something extraordinary about Jesus. So he falls down in the middle of the boat, and says, "Depart from me; I'm a sinner." It is not recorded in Scripture, but I suspect Jesus wanted to say, "Not now, Peter. You can be converted later. We're about to sink. Let's get the boat to shore." What Jesus does say is, "I want you now to be a fisher of people. Save men and women." Peter's experience was a profound sense of his unworthiness before Jesus, and at that moment Jesus commissioned Peter to go forth and share the Good News. Out of the sense of forgiveness comes the call to go forth and to share the good news of the gospel.

The other very touching scene is on the lakeshore after the Resurrection. Peter had denied Jesus three times. Now Jesus takes Peter aside. Jesus doesn't ask him if he is sorry or why he denied him. He asks him three times, "Do you love me?" And each time Peter says, "Yes, Lord, you know I love you." Three times Jesus had Peter say "I'm sorry" through saying "I love you," and each time Jesus said, "Then feed my lambs; feed my sheep." Once you know you're forgiven, you have the power to go forth and share it.

That experience of forgiveness moves us into the Second Week of the Spiritual Exercises. The Second, Third, and Fourth Weeks together are really a process of leading us to a decision of what it means for each one of us, individually, to follow Jesus and to share the Good News. Ignatius invites us to hear the call of Christ and to discern what it means to follow Jesus.

In the Second, Third, and Fourth Weeks, Ignatius invites us to contemplate the life of Jesus. He starts with the Annunciation and goes all the way through to the Resurrection. In the Second Week we contemplate Jesus' mission as portrayed in the Gospels. We enter into the Gospel scenes in a way that helps us grow in the knowledge and love of Jesus. Every time we pray in this Second Week, we pray for the same grace: to know Christ more intimately, to love him more intensely, and to follow him more closely. Or as a song in *Godspell* puts it, "To see Jesus more clearly, love him more dearly, and follow him more nearly, day by day." It's the grace to know, to love, and to follow. The Second Week of the Exercises is about discipleship, which is what Christianity is all about. Discipleship is the call to walk with Jesus, to labor with Jesus, and to bring the world back to God.

The heart of the Second Week is contemplation of the Gospel stories. We enter into them through a kind of imaginative prayer in which we actually enter into the Gospel scene and become part of it. We experience the event with Jesus and the disciples. We become the people in the Gospel story. We are the people healed and forgiven. We are the people fed. We are the disciples feeding people. Praying in this way engages us in the life of Jesus.

Also at the heart of the Second Week is making a decision about how we will live out our lives as disciples in a very specific and concrete way. Each one of us asks, "How is God calling me, in my circumstances, to be of service to others, to be a disciple with Jesus?" We want to find our place in the rhythm of salvation history that is still going on. God is still saving people. The world came from God, and it's going back to God. We're right in the middle of it. We ask ourselves, "How can I labor with Jesus in the work of salvation that is being carried on today? Where am I to be inserted into today's unfolding of God's plan?"

We want the same experience Ignatius had at La Storta: to be placed at the side of Christ and to labor with him to bring the world back to God. The Second Week is all about having your own little La Storta, having your own sense of where God is placing you in following Jesus. This week is central to the experience of the Exercises. It engages our freedom. It challenges us to move from prayer to action to a lived discipleship. It challenges us to know and love Jesus and, ultimately, to follow Jesus.

The Third Week: Sharing in the Suffering and Death of Jesus

The Third Week of the Spiritual Exercises continues the life of Jesus into his passion and his death. We are invited to be with Christ in his passion; we are called to move out of ourselves. In the previous weeks we reflected on our sinfulness with God's love for us and on what God is calling us to do. We have grown to know Jesus better. Now we are invited to go out to Jesus, to be with him in his passion, to move out of ourselves to be united with him in his suffering.

We pray for the grace of sorrow because the Lord is going to his death for our sins. That's how much he loves us. We enter into the mystery of the passion and death of Jesus, which is at the heart of the Christian message.

The Third Week is also what Ignatius calls a time of confirmation. You made a decision in the Second Week about how you are going to follow Jesus. Now Ignatius invites you to take that decision before Christ on the cross, to stand before the crucified Christ and say, "This is my decision." You stand at the foot of the cross and ask, "Can I be, am I going to be, a suffering servant the way Jesus is a suffering servant?"

The Third Week is also a time to ask for strength to be faithful to the decision that you've made. You've made this decision, but maybe you are having second thoughts. The next day you may say, "Wait a minute. What did I do? What have I gotten myself into?" Ignatius puts us in the garden with Jesus struggling with the Father. Jesus asks that the cup of suffering might pass, but in the end, he surrenders to God's will. Like us, the human Jesus struggles with his decision.

In the Third Week we find the strength to live out the decision we've made and to overcome the temptation to go back on a difficult decision.

The Third Week is also a time to deepen our knowledge of Jesus. It's only in the mystery of Jesus' dying and rising that we fully understand who Jesus is. It's only when facing that dying and rising that we understand his mission. It's only in the midst of his dying and rising that we know the depth of our sin and the depth of his love—that Jesus totally emptied himself and gave himself for us. We can't know Jesus until we stand before the cross, because the cross reveals who he is. The love of Jesus is the love that saves us. His love challenges us to be disciples, to take up our cross and follow him. We have to die to "self" so that we can follow him. We find the strength to do so at the foot of the cross.

Above all, at the foot of the cross, we are suddenly overwhelmed with the fact of how much we are loved by God. As Paul says in Romans, it is amazing if a friend gives his or her life for us, but Jesus gave his life for us even when we were sinners. That's how much he loves us. In the Third Week, we let that sink in.

The Fourth Week: Sharing in the Joy of the Risen Christ

The story of Jesus has a happy ending in the Resurrection. In the Fourth Week of the Exercises we are called to be united with Christ in his Resurrection. Ignatius invites us to encounter the risen Christ in the Resurrection appearances.

An interesting footnote in the Exercises gives us a sense of Ignatius's spirituality. He has us pray about all the times the resurrected Jesus appears in Scripture, but the first one is when Jesus appears to his mother. Ignatius adds a note acknowledging that this doesn't appear anywhere in Scripture, but he says that we lack understanding if we don't think that Jesus would first go to his mother after rising from the dead. In other words, if we doubt that this good Jewish boy would go to his mother and say, "Mom, I'm risen," then we don't know Jesus very well. So, this wonderful scene of Jesus appearing to Mary comes first, before all the other times the resurrected Jesus appears.

The grace we pray for in the Fourth Week is to rejoice and be glad at the joy of Jesus. The one we love is now beyond suffering. He is risen. We rejoice that the one we love has been lifted up. Jesus is beyond suffering and death and is once again living the fullness of life.

Again, this grace takes us out of ourselves. Often it's difficult to be happy with someone else, to share someone's joy. Sometimes it's almost easier to be sad with other people. Someone says, "I've had this terrible day," and you say, "I understand." You *do* understand. There's an immediate connection. But when you're having a bad day and somebody says, "I had the greatest day today! Everything is going wonderfully," you sometimes want to say, "I don't want to hear about that. I don't want to be happy right now." It takes a lot of selflessness and generosity to say, "That's terrific! Let's talk about all the wonderful things that happened to you."

The Fourth Week is also a time to experience Jesus as the consoler. That's what the resurrected Jesus is when he appears. The stories always begin with people who are sad and depressed, and Jesus appears and consoles them. Ignatius says that's what Jesus wants to do for us. He wants to console us, to touch our lives and fill them with joy and a sense of expansiveness.

These experiences of the risen Christ also give us a renewed sense of mission. We want to share the Good News. If something wonderful happens to us, we don't just move on to something else. We find someone and say, "Let me tell you about the wonderful thing that has happened." We want to share the joy. We now are coming to the end of the Spiritual Exercises. We are experiencing the joy of Jesus and the disciples, and we are also experiencing the impulse to share it with others. The disciples on the road to Emmaus didn't move on to the next thing after they met Jesus in the breaking of the bread. They ran back to Jerusalem and said, "You can't imagine what happened to us. We met Jesus along the way." So it is with us after we meet the risen Jesus in the Fourth Week.

The Journey to God

The dynamic of the Exercises is to set us free so that we can respond in generosity and love to the call of Christ in our lives. We enter more deeply into the mystery of his dying and rising that is our salvation and the salvation of the world. We enter into the story of Jesus so that his stories will touch our stories and transform them. We are the people in the Gospels.

We are the people who are blind and deaf and hungry and in need of consolation, and Jesus wants to heal and feed and console us.

That's why the Spiritual Exercises are still here after 450 years. Somehow Ignatius captured the paradigm of Christian conversion and the model of the Christian life that we are all called to share. The Spiritual Exercises help us experience that conversion in a structured way so that we come to a profound sense of being loved, forgiven, called, and in union with God. This is the journey to God that is the journey of every Christian. Ultimately, it is the journey of all people. It is an individual journey for each of us with its own unique paths and experiences. It includes our gifts, our life circumstances, and the graced movement of God within us. The Spiritual Exercises are all about God's love: God's love that creates us, God's love that forgives us, God's love that dies for us and rises for us, God's love that saves us, and God's love that calls us to eternal life.

We share this journey together, and that's why the Exercises speak to us and will surely speak to people for hundreds of years to come.

6

The Key Meditations of the Spiritual Exercises

In the previous chapter, we saw how the dynamic of the Spiritual Exercises moves us through the movements of God's love: God's love creating us, forgiving us, calling us, and inviting us to a deeper union by sharing in the dying and rising of Jesus. Much of this occurs through several key meditations. Let's look at how they lead us more deeply into the vision and values of Ignatian spirituality.

The Call of the King

The Call of the King meditation is a transition from the consideration of sin and mercy in the First Week to the reflections on discipleship in the Second Week. This meditation likely has its roots in Ignatius's vision at La Storta. There he saw Jesus carrying his cross and heard the Father say to Jesus, "Take this man [Ignatius] to labor with you." And Jesus turned to Ignatius and said, "Come labor with us." That was a profound experience for Ignatius. It confirmed the direction of his life. He was placed under the standard of Christ, which was a standard of poverty and humility.

Ignatius's vision informed the Call of the King exercise. This exercise is a "consideration." It is not quite a meditation, not quite a contemplation—it is just something to think about. It invites us to our own personal La Storta experience.

Ignatius begins by imagining an earthly king who comes before the people and says, "I want to go out and create a better world and bring peace and bring justice, and I want you all to follow me. It's going to be hard, but in the end we are going to triumph." Ignatius asks us to reflect on that parable and then get in touch with our response. What if someone were to say, "I can assure you, if you work with me for the next six months, that we can eradicate poverty in your city." If you really believe that the person can do this, what happens inside of you? You'd likely feel, "Yes, yes I'll do that. I know it's going to be hard, but I'm willing to do that."

Ignatius wants us to get in touch with the spontaneous generosity and openness and readiness to serve that he believes is in the heart of everyone. He realized that sometimes this is buried deeply. The Call of the King is diagnostic. If you do this consideration and have no desire to serve, no desire to be generous, no desire to do anything further, Ignatius thanks you and says that you can go home now. The rest of the Exercises make sense only in the context of openness, generosity, and the desire to serve.

The Call of the King is intended to stir up that generosity and readiness to serve. Think about Dr. Martin Luther King Jr.'s "I have a dream" speech and the way so many people responded to it. That's what Ignatius wants to capture in this consideration, that passion within all of us. It's a call to a commitment. Then after we are hooked on this king, he tells you that the king actually exists. His name is Jesus, and he's inviting you to bring about the reign of God. Ignatius portrays Jesus as a leader who invites us to share in his lot, to labor alongside him in suffering and glory, and to share in the work of redemption.

This is the answer to the question we ask at the foot of the cross in the First Week of the Exercises: "What should I do for Christ? What ought I to do?" It's the call of the rich young man in the Gospel. Sell everything and come follow me if you want to be perfect. This call focuses the First Principle and Foundation on following Jesus.

In the Call of the King, the grace we pray for is not to be deaf to the Lord's call but to be ready and diligent to accomplish the Lord's most holy will. We pray not to be deaf, to be open, to be ready, and to be generous. That's what we ask of God: "Give me that generous heart so that I can follow you. I want to be part of this plan. I want to bring about this great work that you're involved in."

At this point, Ignatius does not want us to make a decision. We don't know what we're going to do yet. That's going to be worked out in the rest of the Second Week of the Exercises, when we discern what it means for us to walk alongside Jesus. All Ignatius hopes for at this time is for us to get in touch with our desire to go wherever the Lord invites us to go and invites us to follow.

The Call of the King mobilizes our energy. It invites us to get in touch with our dream and to see how Jesus is the fulfillment of our dream. The dream in all of us is to make a better world, a world of peace and justice, a place in which people are honored and respected. Can we share in God's dream for the universe by following Jesus?

For Ignatius, Jesus, who is Creator, Lord, and Savior, is also a leader. Jesus is a living king who is actively at work in the world around us. He is seeking to bring about the reign of

God and is asking us to labor alongside him. We are called to commit to the person of Jesus and to the mission of Jesus.

Ignatius envisioned his own relationship with Jesus in the context of the feudal world of earlier centuries. Ignatius thought of himself as a vassal and of Jesus as the Lord. This was a personal relationship of love and friendship, of entering into and sharing the experience of the other person. It was mutual service. It was fidelity. Jesus for him was his provider, his protector, his leader, and his friend, and Ignatius invites us to relate to Jesus as provider, protector, leader, and friend. It was that kind of personal bond that Ignatius had with Jesus and that he invites us to have as well.

Contemplation on the Incarnation

In the next meditation, Ignatius imagines the three persons of the Trinity up in heaven looking down on the world. The world is a mess. There's evil, there's destruction, everybody's killing one another, there is darkness. The Father, Son, and Spirit are looking down and saying, "What are we going to do about this?" They have a conference, and finally they say, "Somebody ought to go down and straighten it out." So Jesus says, "I'll go." The decision is that the Son will go to become incarnate to save the world.

The final scene he gives is the Annunciation. Mary says yes to God's plan that Jesus will become flesh through her and will come to bring salvation. This contemplation is a wonderful image of the way Ignatius looked at the world. Grace came down from above. Remember his experience at the river Cardoner: everything comes down from above. In the Incarnation, God's grace comes down from above. We see a world in need of salvation; then we see one person, Mary, and the importance of her word and her response to God's plan. Mary is the model for all of us: to say yes to whatever God invites us to do to be part of God's plan.

The contemplation on the Incarnation captures Ignatius's whole vision of the world as a gift from God, the world on its way back to God, and how important each person's response is to that plan: "Will I say yes the way Mary said yes? Will I be open to God's plan in my life, whatever that plan might be?"

The Two Standards

To be part of God's plan, to be a disciple of Jesus, we have to put on the mind and heart of Jesus. We have to put on his values and his attitudes. This brings us to the third of the key meditations—the meditation on the Two Standards.

This meditation is another wonderful example of Ignatius's imagination. He asks us to imagine two great armies: the army of Christ and the army of Satan. In front of each army someone carries a standard, or banner, identifying the group. What he wants us to do is to look at the two standards and meditate on what they represent. In the context of this Second Week of the Exercises, we will make a significant decision about how we're going to serve God. This meditation disposes us to recognize God's will and to discover what keeps us from recognizing it. It gets us to ask ourselves, "What gets in the way?"

The Two Standards are the standard of Christ and the standard of Satan. They represent the struggle between good and evil in the world around us and within our own hearts, the struggle between the forces that lead us toward God and the forces that lead us away from God.

In this contemplation, Ignatius wants us to understand the strategies and the tactics of the forces of good and evil in the world and within our own hearts. So he paints a wonderful, dramatic scene. On one side he has Satan seated on a throne of fire and smoke. It's an image of the fear that takes away our freedom. In the way Ignatius imagines it, Satan sends out all devils and forces of evil to enslave the world. We're terrified of what's going on here. He says that the tactic of the evil spirit is to enslave us, to take away our freedom, to capture our hearts so that they are not open to God. He does that by enticing us to possessions, to great honor, and ultimately to pride.

On the other side, Christ sits in a lowly place: humble, gentle, attractive. Christ sends out disciples to lead people to freedom, to live with detachment, to live in humility. The grace we pray for is to know what keeps us from being free. We ask, "What captures my heart? How am I led to unfreedom in my life?" We also pray to know what sets us free. The grace is to see everything as a gift, so we can be humble and open to God's call.

Ignatius doesn't expect us to say, "Oh, I think I'll go with Satan. I like that vision much more." We've already made a decision to follow Christ. He wants us to understand the contrasting values of Christ and Satan, and how they may be still struggling in our hearts when we come to make our life choice. He wants us to understand the contrast between the values of Jesus and the values of evil. Jesus stands for the values of the Gospel, the Beatitudes, the Sermon on the Mount. He calls us to simplicity, poverty of spirit, compassion, selflessness, the value of life, family, and concern for the needy. We can contrast Jesus' values with the values of consumerism and individualism in our society; the world of manufactured needs; a world of competition that encourages getting ahead at any cost; a world that can disregard the weak, the unattractive, the oppressed; a world of growing narcissism that puts growth, openness, independence, and self-fulfillment ahead of faith, commitment, sacrifice, and responsibility.

These self-centered values are in conflict with the Gospel values of Jesus, who emptied himself, who came to serve us, who came to lay down his life. Jesus is the person for others, the person of compassion who went about helping the poor and the broken. Jesus' values are the values of the Good Samaritan who stops on the road and reaches out in compassion to the man in the ditch. They are the values in the final judgment scene in Matthew when people are asked, "When I was hungry, did you give me something to eat?" These are the values that Ignatius is talking about. He wants us to call them to mind. In following Jesus, we are invited to live out these values, to put on the mind and heart of Jesus. We are called to compassion, to a community of sharing rather than greed, a community of service rather than exploitation, and a community of compassion rather than competition.

These are the contrasting worldviews Ignatius wants us to look at. You should keep that in mind as you go to make your decision. Ask, "Where is my heart? What are the things in the values of darkness that are still pulling at me, that take away my freedom, that lead me away from God?"

The Spiritual Exercises are about making decisions. We can make those decisions on the basis of the values of Jesus and the Gospel, or we can make them on the basis of the values of darkness. We desire to follow Jesus; we've said, "Yes, Lord, I want to follow you. I want to labor beside you." To do that, we have to know the mind and heart of Jesus. We have to know what Jesus values. Only then can we make decisions that carry on Jesus' mission and bring about the reign of God.

Ignatius says that each one of us must discover how to live out those Gospel values in our concrete life circumstances. We ask, "What does it mean for *me* to share in that mission of Jesus? What does it mean for *me* to be a disciple? What does it mean for *me* to walk with Jesus carrying the cross?" That's the challenge that Ignatius puts before us. And it's not easy. It's very demanding.

Throughout the rest of the Second Week, Ignatius has us make a decision. In the Third Week, he invites us to stand before Jesus with our decision and ask ourselves how the decision we have made stands up against the love of Jesus, the love that was willing to go to death. Can you go before the cross with your decision and say, "Yes, I've embraced the values of Jesus, and I want to live out that decision"? That's the confirmation that we seek before the cross. Finally, in the Fourth Week, we are assured that if we embrace these values and follow Jesus, we will also share in his victory.

Let's summarize these three meditations. The Call of the King comes out of the experience of our being forgiven and loved by God. We hear the call, and we ask for the grace not to be deaf to that call. Ignatius then invites us to see how God's plan unfolds in the Incarnation, how God comes down, how Mary is part of that plan, and how we are invited to be part of that plan. Finally, in the Two Standards, Ignatius puts before us the contrasting values of Satan and Christ so we can rightly discern our own call from God.

Contemplation on the Love of God

The final key meditation of the Spiritual Exercises is the Contemplation on the Love of God. I think this contemplation captures the essence of the Ignatian vision and articulates the heart of Ignatian spirituality.

The Contemplation on the Love of God is first of all about God's love for us. It is a call to an intimate knowledge and love and to service of God. It tries to bring us to a place where we can love and serve the Divine Majesty in all things. The grace we pray for is the grace to ask for an interior knowledge deep in our heart of all the great good that we have received. This knowledge elicits profound gratitude. When we really grasp the gifts of God in our life, we are moved to gratitude. Stirred by this gratitude, we are able to serve and love the Divine Majesty in all things, to love and serve God in all things. That's the grace we pray for in this final contemplation.

Ignatius begins the contemplation with two preliminary observations. First, he says that love is expressed in deeds, not just in words. It's not enough just to say nice things to God. The call must be lived out in action. If anything captures Ignatius, it's that sense of always asking, "What do I have to *do*?"

His second observation is that love consists of a mutual giving and sharing of what one possesses. Love is mutuality. As God has given all this to us, we are to give it all to God and to share it with God and with those around us. Through this mutual sharing, the unity of the lover and the beloved comes about.

Ignatius then offers four points for our consideration. He invites us first to call to mind the blessings and favors we have received. We reflect on how much God has done for us, how much God has given us, and how much God desires to give God's very self to us. That moves us to a profound sense of gratitude.

The second point of reflection is how God dwells in what he's given us. God doesn't dump all these gifts on us and say, "You're on your own." God actually dwells in creation, is alive in creation. Above all, God is dwelling in *us*. We are the temple of God. God actually dwells in our hearts.

But there's more. Ignatius's third point is that God labors in creation for us, bringing the world back to God, moving our hearts, trying to move the world toward the reign of God. God is in the world, active in the world, engaged in the world.

Finally, in the fourth point of reflection, Ignatius has us see God's gifts and blessings as coming down from above, so that we will be led back to the source of all good. If everything is a gift, the gift will lead us back to the Giver. And that's where our hearts should finally reside: in God the Giver.

These are not just pleasant thoughts. The purpose of this contemplation is to move us to surrender our hearts back to God. The First Principle and Foundation is about the transcendence of God. This final contemplation focuses on the immanence of God; God is in our midst, in our hearts, in creation. We are called to service and gratitude. These are the two words to remember from Ignatius—*service* and *gratitude*. Gratitude leads us to service.

Ignatius invites us to pray for that deep interior knowledge of the giftedness of creation that moves us to love in return and to render service. It's a movement from thanksgiving to thankfully giving ourselves in service. If Jesus labors for us and with us, we are invited to share the work with him and to bring the reign of God to completion.

Take, Lord, and Receive

This contemplation captures the heart of Ignatian spirituality because it tells us to find God in all things. Where is God? Here, there, and everywhere. God is dwelling here. God is laboring here. By taking the contemplation to heart, we can become "contemplatives in action." This is a phrase coined by Jerome Nadal, one of the early Jesuits who knew Ignatius extremely well. Nadal said that Ignatius was a contemplative in action, a name that's rooted in the Contemplation on the Love of God. As contemplatives in action, we don't pray in the morning and then go out and work. We also pray in the very midst of doing our work. We're contemplatives in the midst of the activity. As we go through our days, we're in touch with God.

The Contemplation on the Love of God sums up the Spiritual Exercises, but it is also a transition out of retreat and back into everyday life. That's where God is—in everyday life. You might want to build three tents and stay on top of the mountain, as the disciples wanted to do when Jesus was transfigured before them. But we can't do that. We've experienced wonderful graces, but it's time to go do something. This is what the angel told the disciples after Jesus ascended to heaven: "Why are you standing here idly looking up to heaven? Go do something." In this contemplation, Ignatius gives us the energy to go forth to find God in our everyday lives and to be of service to one another.

The most famous prayer associated with Ignatius is called the Suscipe. He invites us to say it as part of the Contemplation on the Love of God:

> Take, Lord, and receive all my liberty, my memory, my understanding, and my entire will. You have given all to me. Now I return it. Everything is yours. Do with it what you will. Give me only your love and your grace and that is enough for me.

That's a tough prayer. It is the prayer of surrender. It says, "You have given everything to me. I give it back. Just give me your love and your grace and that's enough for me." It is the total freedom of surrendering everything so that we can follow Jesus and live out the call of the Gospel.

This prayer of total surrender completes the cycle of creation and redemption. All things come from God, and all things go back to God. We give back what we've received. As God has gifted the world in creation and in the Incarnation, so we desire to share in the work of returning that gift, both by personal surrender and by laboring with Christ to bring all things back to God. We want to bring everything back to the Giver of All Gifts.

These meditations are about a call to follow Jesus that's embodied in the concrete life circumstances that we live each day. They are about decisions that are shaped by the Gospel values of Jesus. These decisions enable us to find God in the world and to labor with Jesus to bring the world back to God. This is the movement of Ignatius's Spiritual Exercises—from love to forgiveness to vocation to surrender.

When you come to that moment of surrender, you will find the God you are searching for. You will find God in your everyday life and you will find God in your heart. You're called to be a part of God's great plan. That's the call of Ignatius's prayer for generosity:

> Lord Jesus, teach me to be generous;
> teach me to serve you as you deserve,
> to give and not to count the cost,
> to fight and not to heed the wounds,
> to toil and not to seek for rest,
> to labor and not to ask for reward,
> except that of knowing that I do your
>   most holy will.
> Amen.

7

The Graces of the Exercises

Every person who makes the Spiritual Exercises embarks on a unique spiritual journey. Nevertheless, I think that it's possible to summarize the graces that the Exercises offer in six short sentences:

> We are loved.
> We are gifted.
> We are forgiven.
> We are called.
> We are invited.
> We are sent.

Before we turn to what Ignatius has to say about discernment and decision making, let's briefly consider each of these.

We Are Loved

The most fundamental truth of Christianity is that we are loved unconditionally by God. We are loved from the moment of our conception. We are loved into existence each moment of our lives. If we get that right, then we get Christianity right. If we get that wrong, then we get Christianity terribly wrong. It becomes a frantic, anxious, compulsive attempt to win God's love, not a response of love to someone who has loved us first. We are created out of love, since the very beginning of time.

We are created with a purpose—to know, love, and serve God and to come to eternal life with God forever. We are loved into existence for this reason. Ignatius was clear that we need to know the end for which we are created and recognize that everything else is a means to get there. God seeks a response of love and service from us. We have to keep our hearts set on the goal and be willing to let go of anything that does not take us to the goal. We have to be free.

We Are Gifted

The second grace is the grace of gift. Everything comes as a gift from a loving God. Everything in our experience is connected to the Giver who gave us life, health, family, talents, friends, opportunities, and everything else out of love. We sometimes are tempted to lose touch with the Giver and take things for granted. We presume that things are ours to possess and dispose of in any way we wish. The truth is that everything is a gift.

Ignatius also says that God is present in all these gifts. In fact, God is at work in them. All things reflect God's glory. Everything can lead us to God. The world, then, is sacred, a place "charged with the grandeur of God," in the words of the Jesuit poet Gerard Manley Hopkins.

Our response is reverence, awe, and wonder at the beauty and sacredness of everything, a profound awareness of the presence of God in our lives and in our world, a deep sense of the mystery and gratuity of life. Our most basic response is gratitude. Gratitude is at the heart of Ignatian spirituality. It is the ability to notice and acknowledge the giftedness of life that expands our hearts and impels us to share our gifts with others.

We Are Forgiven

In the Exercises, our reflections on God's love lead us to realize that we have not always been reverent and grateful. We have not always acted as creatures dependent on God. We have not always made choices that lead us to praise, honor, and serve God. We have not always acted as if we believe that we are loved. We have not always treated everything in our lives as a gift.

We come to the humbling awareness that we are sinners, that we have often been ungrateful and unfaithful. We have failed to respond to God's offer of love by failing to love God and love our neighbor. Sin is the failure to bother to love. Sin is not simply the things we do but also the things we fail to do. Ignatius traces all this to a lack of gratitude—failure to recognize everything as a gift to be cherished, fostered, and shared. For Ignatius, ingratitude is the greatest sin and the root of all sin. It is, in the end, the failure to love as God has loved us.

This realization leads us to sorrow. Ignatius invites us to pray for sorrow and shame, for a deep interior knowledge of our sinfulness, of the disorder in our lives, and of our ingratitude and lack of response to God's offer of life. This sorrow leads us to contrition and repentance—a turning toward God, whom we have offended. We realize that we have distanced ourselves from the one we most desire.

We are sinners, but we are forgiven. The two are connected. Only when we claim our sinfulness and stand in sorrow before God can we truly experience God's mercy. We are loved sinners. God loves us even when we are sinners. Only when we know the depth of our sin do we know the depth of God's mercy. We are not as good as we thought, but we are much more loved than we ever imagined. Think of the stories of the prodigal son, the woman caught in adultery, Peter on the lakeshore. The mystic Julian of Norwich said, "The tragedy of life is not that we sin but that we never fully grasp how much we are loved by God." Recall Jesus' final words on the cross, "Father, forgive them. They know not what they do."

We Are Called

The heart of the Gospel is a call to discipleship, to follow Jesus. In the Gospels, no one demonstrates this better than Peter. Two scenes stand out in particular. Both encounters flow out of Peter's awareness of his sinfulness and weakness. In the first he tells Jesus, "Depart from me. I'm a sinner." In the second, on the lakeshore after Jesus' resurrection, Peter says, "Yes, Lord, you know that I love you." Both times Jesus' response is to call Peter to carry on Jesus' ministry: "Be a fisher of people"; "feed my sheep." We hear Jesus' call to follow him when we experience a sense of our sinfulness and God's mercy.

Jesus' call is a call for every Christian. Our experience of being loved and forgiven opens our hearts to that call. Ignatius invites us to hear that call in the meditation on the Call of the King, a parable that can help us to get in touch with our spontaneous generosity and openness and readiness to serve.

We are all called to live out the Gospel values in our lives as committed Christians, in our families and workplace, and in our community.

Ignatius also asks us to contemplate the Trinity looking down on the world in need of redemption and deciding to send the Son to take on human flesh and redeem us. He invites us to contemplate Mary at the Annunciation as she hears God's invitation to become the mother of God. Mary's yes is a model of our own faith response to God's invitation in our lives. Ignatius wants us to hear God's personal invitation to us. *Each one of us* is called—as Abraham was called, as Moses and all the prophets in the Old Testament were called, as the disciples were called. We think of the rich young man who walked away and of Bartimaeus, who followed Jesus along the way. We are loved. We are forgiven. But we are also called.

We Are Invited

After we have heard the words "You are called," Ignatius invites us to get to know Jesus in the Gospel stories. His imaginative contemplation of the Gospels flows from his experience at Loyola during the year of his conversion, when he read a life of Christ that encouraged just such an imaginative engagement with the Gospel stories. As we pray through the

Gospel stories, Ignatius asks us to pray over and over again for one grace: to know Jesus more intimately, to love him more deeply, and to follow him more closely. The words are the words of Ignatius, but he is only echoing the desire and words of God. We are invited to grow in a knowledge and love of Jesus.

Reading the Gospel stories helps us learn the heart of Jesus and try to make it our own. We watch Jesus teach and heal and forgive and feed the people. We experience his kindness and compassion and love for the people. And we know in faith that *we* are those people, that Jesus continues to forgive us and heal us and feed us. In these stories, we go aside with the other disciples to rest a while with Jesus and listen to his concerns and hopes and dreams—and, yes, we go with Jesus to a lonely place to be with him as he prays to his Father. What becomes clear is that Jesus has not just called us to follow; Jesus has also invited us to know him and through him to know his Father. The passion of Jesus' life was to reveal the Father to all of us. This is an invitation to friendship with Jesus and finally a friendship with God. Jesus told the disciples at the Last Supper that he did not call them to be servants but to be friends. That invitation is for all of us. We are all invited to be friends of God.

Friendship has its demands as well. Jesus invites us to friendship, but he also invites us to share in his passion and death. In the third week of the Exercises, Ignatius invites us to share in the sorrow of Jesus, to suffer with him, to be united with him in his passion. Only when we stand before the cross of Christ do we know the depth of our sin and the depth of God's mercy and love for us. We are saved by the love of Jesus, who was willing to give his life to set us free. We cannot know Jesus and understand his mission, we cannot understand who we are called to be, until we are willing to share in his suffering and death and resurrection—the paschal mystery.

We are called to die each day. Dietrich Bonhoeffer wrote, "When Christ calls a person, he bids the person come and die." Jesus said, "Take up your cross and follow me." We must die to our sinfulness and egoism and prejudices. Like Jesus, we have to become suffering servants committed to serve our suffering brothers and sisters, for Christ continues to suffer in our world.

We Are Sent

There is an old spiritual sung in the context of the celebration of Easter. The refrain is "Jesus died and they placed him in a tomb, but that's not how the story ends. He rose. He rose. And that's love. That's love." The death of Jesus is not the end of the story. God raised up Jesus, and that gives us every reason to be people of hope.

In the Fourth Week of the Spiritual Exercises, Ignatius invites us to contemplate the wonderful stories of the appearances of the risen Christ to his disciples. Ignatius asks us to pray for the grace to rejoice with Jesus and his triumph. Jesus appears to his sad and disconsolate disciples, who have in many cases lost hope. He brings them peace and a renewed sense of hope. He consoles them. It is that same risen Jesus who comes to us in moments of darkness and hopelessness and offers us strength and consolation. But Jesus does something else in those encounters. He sends the disciples forth to spread the Good News, to assure others that he is risen and that we, too, will be raised to eternal life. He tells them, "Go tell your brothers and sisters what you have experienced. Go forth to all the nations and proclaim the Good News."

All of this is dramatized in the story of the two disciples on the road to Emmaus. It was Easter Sunday, and the two disciples had left Jerusalem and were on their way to Emmaus when they met Jesus as a stranger on the road. They spoke the poignant words, "We had hoped." They had hoped that the Messiah had come and that the kingdom of God was in their midst, that all God's promises would be fulfilled. But the death of Jesus had put all that into question. Only when

Jesus opened the Scripture to them and shared a meal with them did they recognize him and find renewed hope. Now the disciples' hearts were burning within them. They moved from doubt and loss of hope to the fullness of hope.

They could not contain their joy; they rushed back to share the Good News with the disciples who were in Jerusalem. Their joy and hope gave them a sense of mission, a zeal to tell others about what they had experienced. They were sent forth to carry on the mission of Jesus. It is significant that in this story Jesus does not appear to Peter or Mary or Mary Magdalene or other well-known disciples, but to Cleopas and another unnamed man or woman disciple. They are simply pilgrims going the wrong way. The story assures us that Jesus is present to every pilgrim who is searching for answers, even if he or she is filled with doubt. And those pilgrims become the ones who are to announce the Good News and live out the vision and values of Jesus.

Our baptism commissions us all to carry on the ministry of Jesus, to love and serve our brothers and sisters. At the end of the Spiritual Exercises, we are sent forth to invite others to be part of the kingdom of God. God sends us forth to love others as Jesus has loved us. The final words of Jesus to us are "You are sent."

A Personal Call

God has something unique to say to each one of us. God desires to speak to our hearts—words of love or forgiveness or consolation or encouragement, or words that invite us to share more deeply in his life. He may want to say to us words of challenge and inspiration that call us to live more generously and compassionately and with more love to those around us. God always has a personal word addressed to each one of us.

I have chosen six statements to capture the flow and graces of the Exercises. They are rooted in Ignatius's own experience of God. I believe they are words that God desires to speak to our hearts:

> You are loved.
> You are gifted.
> You are forgiven.
> You are called.
> You are invited.
> You are sent.

When we really hear and believe these words, our hearts will be changed, and our lives will be transformed and filled with the peace that only God can give.

If we know we are loved, we are moved to freely love God and others in return.

If we know we are gifted, we are filled with gratitude that expands our hearts and impels us to share the gifts that God has given us. The desire to share flows from gratitude.

If we know we are forgiven, we will minister in humility and gratitude and will want to share the forgiving love of God with others.

If we know we are called, we will respond in generosity, eager to say yes to God's invitation, always anxious to do more for others, to love with a heart filled with God's love.

If we know we are invited to intimacy and friendship with God, if we know we are called to be friends, not servants, we will respond to Jesus' call to do what he has done, to wash one another's feet. Servants do the master's will. Friends live out the hopes and dreams of God.

If we know we are sent, we will go forth with a sense of mission to carry on the ministry of Jesus and to build God's reign in our world.

8

Discernment

The Spiritual Exercises lead us to greater clarity about the work in life that God has called us to. We've been calling this the dream—God's dream for us, the unique, individual service to God and to others that fulfills our deepest desires. We come now to the practical process of clarifying that dream. We do this through Ignatian discernment and decision making.

All of us, of course, make decisions all the time. Some are very simple decisions; some are very important decisions. Sometimes the decisions are very clear to us. We know exactly what to do. We have a certain confidence about them. But decisions can be difficult. There are conflicting values. There are conflicting responsibilities, and the right path is not clear to us. Ignatius is not concerned about moral decisions between right and wrong. He assumes that we are choosing among morally acceptable alternatives. You may be trying to decide where God is calling you and where God fits into your life. You may be wrestling with tough choices. For example, a family must decide whether to take an elderly parent into the family home or to place him or her in a retirement home. You might be thinking of making a career change to something less financially rewarding but more personally fulfilling. Decisions like these are difficult choices between conflicting values and responsibilities.

Ignatius says that we don't make decisions like these by applying certain laws and structures and principles from which we can deduce the best course. Our history, experience, gifts, desires, feelings, understandings, ideas, inspirations—all of this is part of the work of the Spirit within us. The Spirit is present and at work in our hearts, and we have to reflect on what is going on inside us and in the world around us and allow the Spirit to shape the decisions that we make.

In the Spiritual Exercises, Ignatius offers a rather systematic approach to making life decisions. This approach is one of the most important contributions to Christian spirituality and Christian living that Ignatius made: "How do I follow Jesus? What kind of decisions should I make in my life?" The guidelines Ignatius gives in the Exercises are guidelines that fit our experience in our everyday lives.

God's Hopes and Dreams

Discernment is one of those words that people throw around like *spirituality*. Discernment is an art and a gift. It is a gift of the Holy Spirit, a gift we pray for. I think God gives the gift to everyone, but some people have it to an extraordinary degree. Discernment is the art of discovering God's will for us in the concrete circumstances of our lives. To put it another way, discernment is the discovery of God's hopes and dreams for us, not necessarily God's will. "God's will" sounds rigid and set, written in concrete. God has hopes and dreams for us like a parent does for a child or like we do for our friends. We discover God's hopes in conversation with God.

Discernment is a way of discovering what it means for you, in particular circumstances, to be a disciple of Jesus in your own concrete life situation. Discernment is the art of appreciating the gifts God has given you and discovering how you can best use those gifts to live out your Christian life.

Discernment always occurs in the context of Christian love. It helps us choose the course of action that most authentically answers the deepest desires and longings of our hearts and the movement of the Spirit that God has placed within us. God has hopes and dreams for all of us. They are revealed in creation. They are revealed in the gifts we have. They are revealed in God's word that is spoken to us. They are revealed in our life circumstances. We have to use our freedom to cooperate with God in creating a world that enables us to become the people we want to become and, ultimately, to create the reign of God in a world of peace and justice.

Discernment presupposes that life is a mystery to be lived out, not a problem to be solved. The promptings of the Spirit help us explore that mystery, but life will always remain a mystery. Discernment also presupposes that life is a process of growing in a relationship with God, with the world around us, with the people around us, and ultimately with ourselves.

At the base of Ignatius's approach to discernment is the belief that God touches the individual soul. This is absolutely foundational to Ignatian spirituality and to Ignatian discernment. God does not talk in broad generalities. God is at work in the heart of each person. This conviction is at the heart of what Ignatius means by discernment. There's not some principle that Ignatius gives everyone and then we can deduce whatever we are supposed to do. God is moving in our hearts and in our life circumstances, and we have to listen to that.

Some distinguish between discernment of spirits and discernment of God's will. Discernment of spirits is the discernment of the interior motions of our hearts—the thoughts, feelings, and imaginings that go on inside. It means trying to interpret these so that we can discover what leads us to God and what leads us away from God.

Discernment of God's will is bigger than the discernment of spirits. It includes the discernment of interior emotions of our hearts as well as our life circumstances and certain objective things like the teachings of the church, the word of God, and the consequences that may flow from our actions. It is concerned with the responsibilities and states of life that we may have. Someone may go on a retreat and pray and listen to God's spirit in his heart and come to this profound sense that he is supposed to move away and spend the rest of his life working with the poor. The person then says to his spiritual director, "I'm at peace. This is of God. I know it is of God." And the director says, "What are you going to do with your wife and six kids?" The person says, "Oh, that's not important. I'm at peace." The full discernment of God's will includes consideration of the wife and six kids and other life circumstances. It includes the decisions we have already made. It includes our gifts. There are certain things, objective things, that go into the discernment of God's will.

Rules for Discernment

Ignatius gives us a set of rules or guidelines for discerning the movements of God within our hearts. Discernment is not original to Ignatius. It goes back to the New Testament and to the early desert monks. Ignatius's original contribution was to give us a set of organized, practical guidelines for discernment. They are guidelines, not strict rules that we can apply absolutely.

The rules help us notice what God is doing within us. We don't notice most of this because we are busy with many things. The rules help us notice the interior movements of our hearts, our thoughts, the images that go through our heads, the feelings we have—peace, sadness, openness, and all the others. We want to notice and understand these movements so that we can accept the good ones, the ones that lead us to God, and then reject the bad ones, the ones that lead us away from God.

Ignatius developed the rules for discernment by reflecting on himself. Ignatius's genius was his self-knowledge and self-awareness and the ability to articulate what happened inside him. His understanding of discernment was born at the castle of Loyola. As you recall, while he was recovering from his wounds, he had only two books to read—*Lives of the Saints* and *Life of Christ*. He used to daydream about being a great knight and winning the hand of a lady. Then he read *Life of Christ* and imagined being a knight of God. After several months he began to notice something. Whenever he reflected on being a great knight and winning the hand of a lady, he initially felt terrific, but later he felt sad and empty. When he read *Life of Christ* or *Lives of the Saints* and thought about following Jesus, he was filled with joy and enthusiasm. He noticed that one thing led to sadness and the other led to joy. He began to notice and understand that his feelings were pointing him in the direction that would give him the most joy. The same thing happened to Ignatius at Manresa, and finally in Rome, when he was trying to make decisions about the Society of Jesus. Discernment is about noticing patterns in ourselves and the movements within our hearts.

Ignatius speaks of the promptings of the good spirit and the evil spirit. The good spirit is the Holy Spirit moving within us, the healthy affections that we have in our lives. But he also talks of an evil spirit. This is any force within us that takes us away from God. It may be our subconscious or a personal force of evil. It's that voice inside us that says, "Just roll over Sunday morning. You need a little more rest. You don't need to go to church today." You hear those voices sometimes saying, "Go ahead and take the sixth Krispy Kreme doughnut. Five is okay; six isn't going to make a difference." The evil spirit is the voice inside that leads us astray.

Why are people still using these rules 450 years after Ignatius wrote them? For a simple reason: they work. They describe people's experience. On one level they are just good common sense. On another level they give us wise guidance for following God's call.

Recognizing God's Voice

Let me give you a few examples of the rules. Ignatius says that when we are trying to draw closer to God and to become more holy, prayerful, and loving, the good spirit will encourage us to keep going, and the voice of evil will raise objections and tell us that it is too hard. Ignatius experienced this at Manresa. He was praying seven hours a day, he was talking about God with everybody, and he was just feeling wonderful about his new life. Then this little voice came into his head and said, "This is really pride. You think you're holier than everybody else. Do you really think you can keep doing this for the rest of your life? Do you really think that ten years from now you're going to be doing this? This is crazy. Give it all up. Throw it over. Go back and be a knight." Ignatius realized that this voice was not from God. So he finally stood up and said, "I can't promise I'll do this ten years from now. All I can promise is that I'll do it tomorrow and the next day and the next day." When he rejected the voice, it went away.

In contrast, if we are going away from God and doing things that are not very loving and caring of other people, the evil spirit will encourage us in that behavior. The good spirit will encourage us to move toward God and will stir up our conscience when we move away from God. So, the first rule for discernment is to notice the direction of your life. If you're moving toward God, the good spirit is going to encourage it, and the evil spirit will try to divert you. If you're going away from God, then the evil spirit will encourage that, and the good spirit will try to turn you around.

Ignatius then gives us a set of rules for what to do when we are in desolation. Desolation is sadness, a lack of hope, a sense that God is far away. In desolation, we are not at peace; we are filled with doubts. We begin to say, "I wonder if this makes any sense." Ignatius says that anybody who is trying to move toward God will experience desolation at moments in his or her life. Don't be surprised.

People sometimes make bad decisions when they are in a depressed or desolate state. However, important advice for when we are in desolation is this: Don't make a major life change. Don't set a new direction for your life, because when you are at the bottom of the pit, the voice you're going to hear is the voice of the evil spirit, not the good spirit, and the evil spirit will lead you astray.

Years ago I explained this advice for desolation in an undergraduate class. I said that we often disregard advice about not making a major decision in a time of desolation because we don't like the feeling of desolation. We think we have to change something radically, and then we will feel better. But that's almost always a mistake. I said this in class on a Friday. On Monday, a student named Susan bounded into my office and said, "They work! They work! They work, Father Fagin. They work!" I said, "Calm yourself. What works?" She said, "Those rules you gave us. They work!" She explained that after the Friday class, she went back to her dorm room and found her roommate packing. It was the middle of the semester. The roommate said that she was dropping out of the university. Susan's roommate told her:

> I want to be a doctor. I've always wanted to be a doctor. All my life I've wanted to be a doctor. And I just flunked organic chemistry. I'm never going to be a doctor. It's never going to happen. And then I'm walking back and feeling terrible, and my boyfriend walks up to me. We've been going together for six months. He walks up to me and says right in the middle of everybody, "You know I think we should take some time off. There's this other girl I like." He dumped me right there. I've lost my career. I've lost my boyfriend. I'm leaving.

Susan said to her roommate, "Don't! Don't do that! Don't make a decision in a time of desolation." She explained what I'd said in class about desolation. She said, "Go to the beach for the weekend. Sit on the beach. Enjoy yourself. Relax. Come back on Monday, and then you can make a decision. But don't make it now. Don't make it now. Promise me you won't make it now. You won't drop out of school right now." Her roommate agreed.

Sunday night the girl returned from the beach and told Susan, "You know, you were right. First of all, I never really wanted to be a doctor. That was kind of my parents' idea anyway. I really want to study English literature. I might change my major." She said, "You know that guy? He was a jerk. I am so glad to be rid of that guy." So she said, "I'm staying."

Ignatius gave us other rules, too. He says that we should try to act against desolation by praying more, by being more open, by talking to people, by reaching out. Most of all, we just have to be patient. When we're in the pits, we think that we're never going to get out of it. It's like having the flu. We figure, "I'm going to have this for the rest of my life. I'm going to die with the flu. It will last forever." But of course, the flu doesn't last forever.

Ignatius says that the evil spirit is like a military commander. It searches out our weakness, the places that we're most vulnerable, and that is where it attacks. So we've got to be vigilant. We must know what our weaknesses are so that we're ready when the evil spirit tries to exploit them.

Another very important rule is to stand up to temptation when it happens. I use this example with my students: You're studying hard on Friday night because you need to write a paper. Then somebody knocks on your door and says, "Let's go down to Fat Harry's and have a good time." And you can say, "No, I'm not going to do that. I'm going to work on my paper." The person tells you, "You've got to take some time off. So come on!" And you say, "No, I'm not going. Please leave." And so the person leaves and says, "To heck with you. I'll find someone else to go to Fat Harry's with."

But you can also say, "I don't know. Maybe. Maybe I could take a little time off." Well, the next thing you know, the person is in your room, sitting next to you, and saying, "Yeah, that's right. Come on." Before you know it, you're out the door.

When the evil spirit comes, you have to be very strong at the beginning. Otherwise, you're going to lose the battle. So don't be wishy-washy in the beginning.

Finally, Ignatius says that the evil spirit will always tell us to keep things a secret, not to tell anyone. If we're in the pits and feeling bad and difficult things are going on, we often don't talk to anybody. That's not the voice of God. The moment we hear the voice telling us not to tell anyone, then we can be sure that it is not God's voice. God will always say, "Go to your friends, to somebody you trust. Talk about things."

These are just a few of the rules Ignatius gives. The point of them is to help us listen to what is going on inside, to listen to our feelings, to listen to how God is moving in our hearts, and to begin to interpret that. I can assure you that these rules work. They don't work automatically. They don't work with absolute clarity. We can't solve every problem with these rules. But they are helpful guidelines for noticing the movement of God within our hearts and for interpreting the movements within our hearts to know what leads us toward God.

9

Making Decisions

For Ignatius the discernment of spirits is part of a much broader process of making a decision that includes both objective elements and the more subjective elements of the movements of God within us. Therefore, when a person came to a point in the Exercises at which he or she wanted to make a significant life choice, Ignatius suggested certain procedures for making a decision. Again, he is not concerned with choosing between good and evil. He's concerned with a way of making a choice among alternatives that are all in service to God. The question we have to ask is, "What is God calling me to? Is God calling me to be a priest or religious? Is God calling me to married life? Is God calling me to single life? Is God calling me to be a doctor? Is God calling me to be a teacher?" Ignatius is concerned with those kinds of decisions.

First, Ignatius reminds us that we must make decisions in light of the end for which we were created. He goes back to the First Principle and Foundation at the beginning of the Spiritual Exercises. What is the purpose of our lives? Why are we here? If we're going to make a decision, it's very important that we put the goal first. The goal is to praise, reverence, and serve God. The goal is to be a disciple of Jesus and to live out the Christian life. The question is how we will do that.

Ignatius says that people often make decisions backward. They say, "I want to do this. Now how can I do this and somehow praise, reverence, and serve God? How can I work the means around to the end?" Ignatius says that we should instead start with the end. The end is being a disciple of Jesus: "What does it mean for me to love as Jesus loved?" The most challenging line in all of Scripture is "Love one another as I have loved you." What could be more challenging? That makes the Golden Rule look like a piece of cake. This love of altruism and self-sacrifice is our goal. Ignatius wants us to reflect first on why we are here and what the purpose of our life is. Then in that context, we choose the best means to get there.

Three Ways to Make a Decision

Ignatius talks about three ways to make a decision. These are not completely separate. They overlap, and they double back and forth, but he presents them separately.

The first way happens when the decision is perfectly clear. This is wonderful when it happens. We don't have any doubt about what we're supposed to do. We know what God wants, and we have real peace about it. This is Matthew sitting at his little tax table when Jesus walks up and says, "Come follow me." Matthew doesn't need to discern the decision to do so. He gets up and follows Jesus. Paul gets knocked to the ground, and the voice comes from heaven, "Saul, Saul, why are you persecuting me?" He didn't have to discern that. This is pretty clear. There are moments like these when decisions are clear, and we just know in our deepest hearts that there is a right thing to do. We think, "This is what I should do." We are always hoping for and looking for that kind of clarity.

More often, though, the decision isn't so clear. We find ourselves pulled in different directions. Something sounds like a good idea, and then it does not. First one choice seems better and then another. That's when we need the rules for discernment to help us listen to what is going on in our hearts so that we can discover what's taking us to God and what's taking us away from God.

Ignatius expected that most people making significant life decisions would be in some conflict. He tells directors of the Spiritual Exercises not to worry if someone is in emotional turmoil; the only people to worry about are the people in whom nothing is happening. Ignatius expected us to move from consolation to desolation when we are trying to make a significant decision because good and evil spirits will be at work. For example, a man went on a retreat and felt a call to be a permanent deacon. He spent months going back and forth with the decision. Sometimes he thought, "Yes, that is what God wants me to do." Then questions arose about what the commitment would mean for his family. How much time would he be away from his home? Back and forth. He was at peace at one moment about it, and then doubts would arise. It took him a long time to sift through what was going on in his heart so he could finally come to some peace.

The third way to make a decision is when we are basically at peace. There are no strong movements one way or the other. When that happens, we can use our reason and our imagination. We are at balance. We're open. We can honestly ask God, "Where do you want me to go? What are you asking me to do?"

When we are in that state, Ignatius gives us two suggestions. One is to bring the decision before God and simply write down the pros and cons. We can write down what the reasons are for and against one option, and then do the same for the other alternative. We can sit there and look at the decision rationally. It's amazing how that can clarify things. Instead of bouncing from one reason to another, we can write them down and then pray with them. This method uses our reason.

Ignatius's other suggestion is to use our imagination. He gives a couple of techniques for us to do that. First, when you have to make a serious decision, imagine a friend coming to you with that same decision and saying, "Gee, I don't know what to do. Should I do this or should I do that?" What advice would you give to your friend? This helps you step back and be more objective. You tell your friend what the right choice might be; it may be the right choice for you, too. Often we are great at giving advice to other people. We give good advice, but we're terrible at giving it to ourselves.

Another technique is to imagine ourselves on our deathbed or at the Day of Judgment standing before God. Which choice would we wish we had made? This takes us away from the satisfaction of the moment to look at the big picture and ask, "Where is God calling me?" When we come to our deathbed and look back at our life, we're probably going to say that we wish we had made the more loving, the more giving, the more caring choice.

The Whole Person Decides

Any important decision will likely include all of these methods. They all call on your feelings. We use our reason to reflect on the pros and cons. We use imagination as we consider different scenarios. Ignatius believed that if we want to make a good decision, we do it as a whole person. We don't just figure it out rationally. We don't just follow our feelings, and we don't just follow our imagination. We need all of these things to work together.

Ignatius gives these methods to spiritual directors and encourages them to use them flexibly. So with some people, directors might really want to focus on the imagination. With other people, reason might be much more important. They might be thinkers who really need to look at the pros and cons. Other people might really need the affective side. In the end, we need all parts of ourselves.

Once we have made a decision, we bring the decision to God for confirmation. This is the step that most people skip. We make a decision, and we feel so relieved that we just want to do it. If we go to a friend, our friend might say that we have made a dumb decision. We don't want to hear that.

Ignatius invites us to take our decision to God. He even says to take it to the foot of the cross and say, "Lord, this is what I've decided to do. How do you feel about it?" Can we be at peace presenting this decision to God? Can we feel that this is the loving thing to do? Are we really happy with this? Can we look at the infinite love of God and say that this is the decision that we are comfortable with? Confirmation is a very important part of the decision-making process. It is asking God to really affirm the decision.

The Elements of a Good Decision

To make a good decision, the first thing we need to do is pray. By prayer I don't mean a prayer like "God help me. God help me. God help me." We need to listen, to bring an open heart before God. Listen to the Spirit. Ask for the grace to be open and hear God's call in your life.

Second, we need to get good information about the various options. Know the facts and the implications of those facts. Also, know what the alternatives are. Sometimes we're torn between two things, and there is a third way that has the values of both. So gather the information.

The third element is to reflect on our affective responses in relationship to God. We need to notice, interpret, and reflect on the feelings of peace and the lack of peace, the feelings of joy and the lack of joy, the feelings that increase our faith and the ones that darken our faith. Fourth, we need to reflect on all that, and then weigh the options, the pros and cons. In his diary Ignatius records what happened while he was making an important decision regarding the Jesuits. Every morning he was having extraordinary mystical experiences, but he also sat down and wrote out all the pros and cons. He saw that as part of the decision, too. Doing so is necessary to balance our heads and our hearts because our feelings and thoughts work together.

The final step is bringing the decision to God for confirmation.

So these are the steps: pray, get good information, listen to the Spirit moving in your heart, use your head to decide the pros and cons, make a decision, and bring it to God for confirmation.

Decision making is not automatic. It's a process. There is a lot that goes into that process, and we may not come to absolute certitude. There's still mystery in it. We make the best decision we can make given the time we have. Ignatius was concerned about action. He was concerned about how to live out the experience of being loved, of being forgiven, of being called by God. He did not have a magic method that leads to absolute certitude. What Ignatius offers us is the wisdom of his own experience, what he learned from his own life and from dealing with others: the way that God shapes the human heart, the way that God reveals to us God's hopes and dreams for us, the belief and the trust that God will finally lead us the way that God wants us to go, and that we will finally discover that the deepest desires of our hearts are the deepest desires of God's heart. We will not get to our deepest desires and discover that God has radically different desires. The struggle is to get to those deepest desires and live them out. If we do that, then that's when we find peace. We know that we've heard God's call.

10

Our Deepest Desire

The path to discipleship that Ignatius laid out may seem challenging, even daunting. He wants us to come to freedom so that we can hear God's call and respond to it in total generosity. He wants us to surrender to God in everything in absolute trust. He wants us to find God in our lives each day. He wants us to follow Christ in his suffering and death. That seems pretty daunting for people who live in the world each day in the midst of the human demands of family, work, and everyday responsibilities. Is what Ignatius asks realistic? Is it some ideal that is so far beyond us that we'll never be able to understand it or achieve it? We may have the feeling sometimes that we have been asked to do a pole vault, and Ignatius has put the bar at twelve feet when we have a six-foot pole. We say,

"I'm sorry. I just can't do that. It's impossible. It's a nice ideal, but what does it have to do with my life?"

It has everything to do with our lives. Ignatius does offer an ideal, one that we will never fully achieve in this life; but more importantly, he offers us a direction. He describes a Christian journey that leads to life and to happiness. It is a call to freedom. It is a call to discipleship. It is a call to share in the saving event of the dying and rising of Jesus. It is a call to mission in the midst of the world.

Ignatius describes God's desire for us, God's hope for us, God's dream for us—a dream to lead us from freedom to love to life. What Ignatius describes is what our hearts long for, the deepest desires of our hearts, the fulfillment of the restlessness of our hearts, a restlessness that leaves us always wanting more.

No one can ever say, "I have finished the Spiritual Exercises." We're always struggling to be free, to love, and to follow Jesus more closely. We're always struggling to let go. We're struggling to surrender to God. That's the story of our lives. What Ignatius describes shouldn't discourage us. The Spiritual Exercises are an invitation to grow into who we are called to be. We walk the journey in humility and hope because we know that the journey is the work of God's grace within us. It is God's work, and that's where we put the trust. We walk the journey of humility and hope because no matter how halting our steps or how many detours we take or side roads we travel, we know that this is the road that leads to the goal of our lives and the deepest desires of our hearts.

What Ignatius offers is not so much an ideal. It's an invitation, the invitation of Jesus to follow, to always strive for what Ignatius called *magis*, which means always striving for more, always trying to grow more. We need not worry about an impossible ideal put before us if each day we strive with God's help to be more free, more grateful, more generous, more loving, more in tune with the heart of Jesus. If we strive each day to be more attentive and more responsive to God in our lives, that's what he invites us to. That's God's hope for us, and it is the deepest desire of our hearts.

Editor's Note

This book is based on a series of lectures that Fr. Gerald Fagin, SJ, delivered to students and staff at Loyola University New Orleans, where he was associate professor of theology at the Loyola Institute for Ministry. The lectures struck a chord with the university community. They were transcribed, lightly edited, and published in a pamphlet that found an enthusiastic local audience.

In 2012, editors at Loyola Press began talking to Fr. Fagin about developing this material into a small book. He liked the idea and I began working with him on the project. I had been his editor on his book *Putting on the Heart of Christ: How the Spiritual Exercises Invite Us to a Virtuous Life*, and we had an excellent relationship. By May 2012, we had finalized a plan for the book. I was going to rearrange and edit the previously published material. Jerry was going to spend part of the summer writing new material, mainly about personal discernment.

Sadly, Jerry became gravely ill that spring and died in June. He was not able to do any of the writing he had hoped to do. I finished the book according to the plan he and I had worked out. The manuscript was reviewed by Fr. Mark Thibodeaux, SJ, and Judy Deshotels, two close friends of Jerry who knew his work well. We are confident that this book presents what he wanted to say. However, we are mindful that it doesn't contain *everything* he wanted to say.

Jerry Fagin was a beloved teacher, a penetrating thinker, and a friend. May this book, his last, give him honor and bring the blessings of Ignatian spirituality to many.

Jim Manney

Loyola Press

About the Author

Gerald M. Fagin, SJ, was a spiritual director for over 35 years. He taught courses in spirituality and moral theology in the Loyola Institute for Ministry graduate program at Loyola University New Orleans.

Other Ignatian Titles

The Ignatian Adventure
Experiencing the Spiritual Exercises
of St. Ignatius Loyola in Daily Life

$14.95 • Pb • 3577-1

God Finds Us
An Experience of the Spiritual
Exercises of St. Ignatius Loyola

$9.95 • Pb • 3827-7

A Simple, Life-changing Prayer
Discovering the Power of
St. Ignatius Loyola's Examen

$9.95 • Pb • 3535-1

To order: call **800.621.1008**,
visit **www.loyolapress.com/store**,
or visit your local bookseller.

LOYOLA PRESS.
A JESUIT MINISTRY

3441 N. Ashland Avenue
Chicago, Illinois 60657
(800) 621-1008
www.loyolapress.com

Cover art credit: Dr. Cloud/Shutterstock.com.

ISBN-13: 978-0-8294-3833-8
ISBN-10: 0-8294-3833-5
Library of Congress Control Number: 2013937783

Printed in the United States of America.
13 14 15 16 17 18 Versa 10 9 8 7 6 5 4 3 2 1

Discovering Your Dream

How Ignatian Spirituality Can
Guide Your Life

Gerald M. Fagin, SJ

LOYOLA PRESS.
A JESUIT MINISTRY

Chicago